D. H. Lawrence

Titles in the series Critical Lives present the work of leading cultural figures of the modern period. Each book explores the life of the artist, writer, philosopher or architect in question and relates it to their major works.

In the same series

Hannah Arendt *Samantha Rose Hill*
Antonin Artaud *David A. Shafer*
John Ashbery *Jess Cotton*
Roland Barthes *Andy Stafford*
Georges Bataille *Stuart Kendall*
Charles Baudelaire *Rosemary Lloyd*
Simone de Beauvoir *Ursula Tidd*
Samuel Beckett *Andrew Gibson*
Walter Benjamin *Esther Leslie*
John Berger *Andy Merrifield*
Leonard Bernstein *Paul R. Laird*
Joseph Beuys *Claudia Mesch*
Jorge Luis Borges *Jason Wilson*
Constantin Brancusi *Sanda Miller*
Bertolt Brecht *Philip Glahn*
Charles Bukowski *David Stephen Calonne*
Mikhail Bulgakov *J.A.E. Curtis*
William S. Burroughs *Phil Baker*
Byron *David Ellis*
John Cage *Rob Haskins*
Albert Camus *Edward J. Hughes*
Fidel Castro *Nick Caistor*
Paul Cézanne *Jon Kear*
Coco Chanel *Linda Simon*
Noam Chomsky *Wolfgang B. Sperlich*
Jean Cocteau *James S. Williams*
Joseph Conrad *Robert Hampson*
H.D. (Hilda Doolittle) *Lara Vetter*
Salvador Dalí *Mary Ann Caws*
Charles Darwin *J. David Archibald*
Guy Debord *Andy Merrifield*
Claude Debussy *David J. Code*
Gilles Deleuze *Frida Beckman*
Fyodor Dostoevsky *Robert Bird*
Marcel Duchamp *Caroline Cros*
Sergei Eisenstein *Mike O'Mahony*
Frantz Fanon *James S. Williams*
William Faulkner *Kirk Curnutt*
Gustave Flaubert *Anne Green*
Ford Madox Ford *Max Saunders*
Michel Foucault *David Macey*
Benjamin Franklin *Kevin J. Hayes*
Sigmund Freud *Matthew ffytche*
Mahatma Gandhi *Douglas Allen*
Antoni Gaudí *Michael Eaude*
Jean Genet *Stephen Barber*
Allen Ginsberg *Steve Finbow*
Johann Wolfgang von Goethe *Jeremy Adler*
Günter Grass *Julian Preece*
Ernest Hemingway *Verna Kale*
Langston Hughes *W. Jason Miller*
Victor Hugo *Bradley Stephens*
Zora Neale Hurston *Cheryl R. Hopson*
Aldous Huxley *Jake Poller*
J.-K. Huysmans *Ruth Antosh*
Christopher Isherwood *Jake Poller*
Derek Jarman *Michael Charlesworth*
Alfred Jarry *Jill Fell*
James Joyce *Andrew Gibson*
Carl Jung *Paul Bishop*
Franz Kafka *Sander L. Gilman*

Frida Kahlo *Gannit Ankori*
Søren Kierkegaard *Alastair Hannay*
Yves Klein *Nuit Banai*
Arthur Koestler *Edward Saunders*
Akira Kurosawa *Peter Wild*
D. H. Lawrence *David Ellis*
Lenin *Lars T. Lih*
Jack London *Kenneth K. Brandt*
Pierre Loti *Richard M. Berrong*
Rosa Luxemburg *Dana Mills*
Jean-François Lyotard *Kiff Bamford*
René Magritte *Patricia Allmer*
Gustav Mahler *Stephen Downes*
Stéphane Mallarmé *Roger Pearson*
Thomas Mann *Herbert Lehnert and Eva Wessell*
Gabriel García Márquez *Stephen M. Hart*
Karl Marx *Paul Thomas*
Henri Matisse *Kathryn Brown*
Guy de Maupassant *Christopher Lloyd*
Herman Melville *Kevin J. Hayes*
Henry Miller *David Stephen Calonne*
Yukio Mishima *Damian Flanagan*
Eadweard Muybridge *Marta Braun*
Vladimir Nabokov *Barbara Wyllie*
Pablo Neruda *Dominic Moran*
Friedrich Nietzsche *Ritchie Robertson*
Georgia O'Keeffe *Nancy J. Scott*
Richard Owen *Patrick Armstrong*
Octavio Paz *Nick Caistor*
Fernando Pessoa *Bartholomew Ryan*
Pablo Picasso *Mary Ann Caws*
Edgar Allan Poe *Kevin J. Hayes*
Ezra Pound *Alec Marsh*
Sergei Prokofiev *Christina Guillaumier*
Marcel Proust *Adam Watt*
Sergei Rachmaninoff *Rebecca Mitchell*
Arthur Rimbaud *Seth Whidden*
John Ruskin *Andrew Ballantyne*
Jean-Paul Sartre *Andrew Leak*
Erik Satie *Mary E. Davis*
Arnold Schoenberg *Mark Berry*
Arthur Schopenhauer *Peter B. Lewis*
Dmitry Shostakovich *Pauline Fairclough*
Adam Smith *Jonathan Conlin*
Susan Sontag *Jerome Boyd Maunsell*
Gertrude Stein *Lucy Daniel*
Stendhal *Francesco Manzini*
Igor Stravinsky *Jonathan Cross*
Rabindranath Tagore *Bashabi Fraser*
Pyotr Tchaikovsky *Philip Ross Bullock*
Dylan Thomas *John Goodby and Chris Wigginton*
Leo Tolstoy *Andrei Zorin*
Leon Trotsky *Paul Le Blanc*
Mark Twain *Kevin J. Hayes*
Richard Wagner *Raymond Furness*
Alfred Russel Wallace *Patrick Armstrong*
Simone Weil *Palle Yourgrau*
Tennessee Williams *Paul Ibell*
Ludwig Wittgenstein *Edward Kanterian*
Virginia Woolf *Ira Nadel*
Frank Lloyd Wright *Robert McCarter*

D. H. Lawrence

David Ellis

REAKTION BOOKS

In memoriam: Mark Kinkead-Weekes

Published by Reaktion Books Ltd
Unit 32, Waterside
44-48 Wharf Road
London N1 7UX, UK

www.reaktionbooks.co.uk

First published 2025
Copyright © David Ellis 2025

All rights reserved

No part of this publication may be reproduced, stored in a retrieval system, or transmitted, in any form or by any means, electronic, mechanical, photocopying, recording or otherwise, without the prior permission of the publishers

Printed and bound in Great Britain by Bell & Bain, Glasgow

A catalogue record for this book is available from the British Library

ISBN 978 1 83639 013 8

Contents

1 Lawrence before Frieda   7
2 Turning Point   25
3 *The Rainbow*   40
4 Cornwall and *Women in Love*   55
5 Orphans of the Storm   73
6 A Busy Time!   87
7 A Wider World   107
8 There and Back   123
9 *Lady Chatterley's Lover*   141
10 Towards the End   160

References   179
Select Bibliography   187
Photo Acknowledgements   191

D. H. Lawrence, 1915.

1
Lawrence before Frieda

D. H. Lawrence was the first great writer to emerge from the English proletariat. His father began working down a coal mine around 1856, when he was only ten years old, and was still doing so in his mid-sixties. Arthur Lawrence and his wife raised their family in an expanding mining town called Eastwood, which is built on and around a steep hill 16 kilometres (10 mi.) to the northwest of Nottingham. They had five children, of whom David Herbert was the fourth (he had both a younger and an older sister as well as two older brothers). Within his family, and among his friends, he was always known as Bert and felt embarrassed by his first name. In a reminiscence of his early days, he records how the headteacher of his infant school angrily reproached him for not wanting to be called David, which he insisted – no doubt thinking of the Bible – was 'the name of a great and good man'.[1]

Lawrence's mother, Lydia Lawrence, was a stranger to the Eastwood area. She had been brought up in Kent in a marginally more cultivated environment than that of her future husband, and always spoke standard English rather than the local dialect. Her way of speaking became part of her effort to ensure that her children did well in life, and one of its consequences was that they became bilingual, talking with her at home in a way that was recognizably middle class but able also to join in dialect conversations with their father, or friends in the school playground. Towards the end of his life, when Lawrence had abandoned the powerful emotional allegiance he initially felt towards his mother and had begun to sympathize with his father, he expressed in verse the dilemma he

The Lawrence family, *c.* 1895.

felt at having two ways of speaking available to him as a child. He describes his mother in these verses as a 'superior soul', 'cut out to play a superior role/ in the god-damn bourgeoisie', and goes on:

> We children were the in-betweens
> little non-descripts were we,
> indoors we called each other *you*,
> outside, it was *tha* and *thee*.[2]

By entitling his poem 'Red-herring', in allusion to the proverbial expression 'neither fish, nor flesh, nor good red herring', Lawrence suggests that it has been a disadvantage to be caught between two cultures. As far as his writing is concerned, however, there is much to indicate that the opposite was true.

Lydia Lawrence's ambitions for her children concentrated at first on her second son, Ernest. A clever schoolboy, he began clerical work in the local area but then secured a post in a London office and appeared to have a prosperous business or professional career ahead of him. One of the very many excellently written scenes in the early part of D. H. Lawrence's *Sons and Lovers* describes the excitement of the whole family when a figure based very closely on Ernest comes home from London at Christmas, laden with presents. But in 1901, when he was only 23, Ernest fell suddenly ill with erysipelas and died. The effect on his mother was devastating, and she took a long time to recover.

Bert Lawrence found it irritating when he was told at school that he would never be as good as his brother Ernest, but he did well enough to pass the examination qualifying him for entry to Nottingham's grammar school. When he was fifteen, he left school for a job as a clerk in a surgical-goods factory, but he had never been robust and, not long afterwards, contracted pneumonia and became very seriously ill. For those who, like Lawrence, were characterized by people around them as having a 'weak chest', the great fear and danger was tuberculosis (TB), the major cause of early death in all the regions of Great Britain, as well as in Europe, at this time. He was tenderly looked after by his mother – brought

Lawrence's birthplace, Victoria Street, Eastwood.

out of the torpor Ernest's death had caused and desperate not to lose another son – and spent a lengthy period of convalescence with her at home. It was no doubt during this period that the bond between mother and son strengthened to a point that Lawrence would later recognize as unhealthy. When in 1910 his mother was dying an agonizingly slow death from cancer, he explained to a friend that his relation to her had been almost like that of a husband to his wife, and that they were so attuned they never needed words. 'It has been rather terrible,' he added, 'and has made me, in some respects, abnormal.'[3]

As D. H. Lawrence started to recover from pneumonia, his mother began looking for ways to rebuild his strength, and one opportunity came from a woman called Ann Chambers, whom she met regularly at the Congregational chapel they both attended. The husband of Mrs Chambers had recently begun to rent a small farm 5 kilometres (3 mi.) outside Eastwood, and she invited Lydia Lawrence and her convalescent son to visit her there. This was why, one day in the summer of 1901, mother and son took the cross-country walk to the Haggs, as the farm was called, and Lawrence was introduced to the whole Chambers family. At this time, the landscape around Eastwood was dotted with the winding gear that took men like Arthur Lawrence down into the various pit shafts: 'My father was a working man/ and a collier was he,' Lawrence jauntily wrote in 'Red-herring', 'at six in the morning they turned him down/ and they turned him up for tea.' Arthur Lawrence could walk to his work at Brinsley Colliery from Eastwood through the countryside, and he passed on both an appreciation and intimate knowledge of nature to his children. The boy who accompanied his mother to the Haggs had therefore lots to observe on the way there, but of course he learned a great deal more about the natural world as he became intimate with the whole Chambers family and eagerly participated, wherever he could, in work on the farm.

An important characteristic of Lawrence, which is often forgotten in discussions of him as a pioneer in his dealings with sex, is how socially attractive and outgoing he could be. As his visits to the Haggs steadily increased, so much so that there would come a point when his mother would sarcastically complain that he might as well sleep there, he became an essential part of Chambers family life. They loved his enthusiasm and the energy he brought to helping around the farm or inventing and then participating in party games. Like so many other novelists, he was an accomplished mimic and could make them all laugh with imitations of various

Eastwood public figures whom he found pompous. Overflowing with speculations that he invited them to discuss, he brought with him titles of books he had recently read or discovered. They were all readers, but none more so than Jessie, the second of the Chambers girls and the fifth of seven children. A year and a half younger than Lawrence, she was a deeply serious girl who read as voraciously as he did, so that the two adolescents developed a strong relationship based predominantly on their shared literary and intellectual interests. When Lawrence began to think that he himself might one day like to write, it was to Jessie, and only Jessie, that he showed his first attempts.

After his recovery from illness, Lawrence did not go back to the factory but instead began training as a teacher. He started as a teaching assistant in a local primary school but was then allowed to attend courses at a special training centre which had been established in the nearby town of Ilkeston. In his day, teaching was becoming a common means of social mobility for children from the working or lower-middle classes: a little later, Jessie Chambers would also begin teacher training, as would Lawrence's younger sister, Ada. There were a number of both male and female friends with whom he was reunited at Ilkeston or got to know there. As they grew into their late teens and early twenties, these young people constituted a lively group, always ready to consider new ideas, and became a valuable addition to the contacts Lawrence had already made through his regular attendance at the Congregational chapel. When T. S. Eliot once referred contemptuously to the poverty of the intellectual milieu in which Lawrence developed, F. R. Leavis responded by noting that, while Lawrence may not have had Eliot's advantage of Harvard and then Oxford, there was plenty to nourish the mind in the Eastwood of the day. It became clear that his was a mind that deserved nourishing when he took one of the nationwide examinations in which his training at Ilkeston culminated and was placed in the top category. A little later, he took another examination which made it possible for him to begin a two-year teacher training course at what is now Nottingham University.

Jessie Chambers (1887–1944).

Lawrence was not especially impressed by those who taught him at Nottingham, but by that point his efforts to become a writer occupied an increasingly large amount of his energies. By the time he had qualified, as a primary or elementary rather than secondary school teacher, he had written a good deal, including a version of the novel which would eventually appear as *The White Peacock*. But there was nothing as yet to indicate he could ever make his living by writing, and once he had completed his studies he was anxious to find a teaching post quickly, in part so that he could begin to compensate his family for the considerable financial sacrifices they had made in supporting him while he was a student (his father was fond of reminding his mother how much good money Bert

D. H. Lawrence, the young author.

could have earned had he gone down the pit once he left school). At first, none of his applications bore fruit, but then he was invited to present himself at a new school in Croydon, about 15 kilometres (9 mi.) south of London, and he made a sufficiently good impression to be taken on there.

While in 1908–9 Lawrence was learning how to control classes of more than fifty young boys, Jessie Chambers was mulling over his writing. Both she and Lawrence had been impressed by a new literary journal that had recently begun to appear, which carried contributions from the leading writers of the day, including Joseph Conrad and Thomas Hardy. It was called the *English Review*, and its editor was Ford Madox Hueffer, who changed his last name to Ford at the end of the First World War. He had publicized his willingness to consider contributions from new young writers, and Jessie therefore sent him a few of Lawrence's poems. Impressed by what he saw, Hueffer asked how he could contact Lawrence and invited him to call at his London office. Once the two had met, and Hueffer realized how much this young man had already written in addition to his poetry, he was quick to feel, and publicly declare, that he had discovered a genius.

An example of the early prose writing that gave rise to this compliment was the initial version of a short story entitled 'Odour of Chrysanthemums'. This tells the tale of a young mother waiting for her husband to return from the pit and growing ever more angry and resentful as she assumes he has stopped off to spend his money in the pub, as usual. But the long delay is in fact a consequence of his having been trapped by the collapse of the roof of the shaft in which he was working, and some of his colleagues eventually carry his dead body into the woman's cottage. In his treatment of the episode, Lawrence is recalling what he had heard of how one of his paternal uncles had died (all his father's brothers had been miners), and a detail which must have been part of family lore: that because the roof had not fallen on him directly, and he had therefore died of suffocation, his dead body was relatively unblemished. The details of the woman's life as she waits for her husband's return are brilliantly evoked, as are those which describe how she and her mother-in-law later wash his corpse. Hueffer pointed out that the reading public of the time probably knew more about the lives of tribes in Central Africa than those of miners from the Midlands, and urged Lawrence along the path of realistic depiction of what he knew best. Lawrence would later use the situation in 'Odour of Chrysanthemums' for a play he called *The Widowing of Mrs Holroyd*, one of ten he wrote during his career.

Lawrence's professional relationship with Hueffer was significant for his first novel, *The White Peacock*. After numerous rewritings, Lawrence finally showed the novel to Hueffer, who was sufficiently impressed to recommend it to William Heinemann. *The White Peacock* was first published by Heinemann in December 1910 and based on a familiar love triangle. The high-spirited, skittish Lettie is courted by Leslie Tempest, who is from a local 'county' family, but she is more physically attracted to a young farmer, George, who is less well-off and not so well educated. Lettie chooses to marry Leslie nonetheless, while George marries a good-natured working-class woman who inherits a local pub. Never able to forget Lettie, he begins drinking himself to death. Since Lettie also finds marriage to Leslie unsatisfying, the story is not an especially uplifting one. It is seen chiefly through the eyes of her brother Cyril, who is, as Jessie Chambers complained, a far too indefinite and colourless figure.[4] Most of the other characters are very recognizably based on people from Lawrence's immediate environment – Lettie on his young sister Ada, for example, and George on Jessie's brother Alan. But a major difference from real life is that Cyril, Lettie and their mother – the father is mostly absent, and when he does return home conveniently dies – are distinctly genteel and inhabit a comfortable middle-class environment. When they talk together, sometimes interspersing their remarks with quotations from French or Latin, they can sound remarkably pretentious and stilted. It took Lawrence some time to be able to create educated middle-class characters who could converse with one another as believably as the wife and mother-in-law in *The Widowing of Mrs Holroyd*, yet it seems as if when he first began *The White Peacock*, as early as 1906, he assumed it would not find readers unless it reflected back to them their own social environment.

One of the two major distinguishing features of Lawrence's first novel is the abundance and detail of its descriptions of the countryside: the depth of his knowledge of and warm appreciation for the natural world are evident throughout, so much so that one can sometimes feel that a setting means more to him than the human action taking place within it. The second is its eroticism. Characters who are attracted to each other are consistently described in ways which make it clear that they are aware of, or troubled by, each other's bodies. This is certainly true not only of the heterosexual couples, but of Lawrence's treatment of relations between men. In one chapter called 'A Poem of Friendship', he describes how Cyril and George go swimming together and how George takes hold of Cyril to dry him with a towel 'as if I were a child, or rather, a woman he loved': 'I left myself quite limply in his hands, and, to get a better grip of me, he put his arm round me and pressed me against him, and the sweetness of the touch of our naked bodies one against the other was superb.'[5] When E. M. Forster, an avowed if at that period non-practising homosexual, first read *The White Peacock* much later, he claimed that Lawrence did not have 'a glimmering from first to last of what he was up to'.[6] At this early point in Lawrence's writing career, it may well have been the case that he was not aware of his own bisexuality or the way it made itself known in his work. Certainly, he describes the sexual chemistry between Lettie and Leslie, between her and George and between Cyril and Emily (George's sister and a very recognizable portrait of Jessie Chambers) in ways which, like 'A Poem of Friendship', suggest how unaware he was of the raised eyebrows they might cause in some quarters. The tangle of relationships in the novel makes its theme the conflict between the intellectual and the physical, the spirit and the flesh. Lawrence introduces at one point a gamekeeper called Annable, who is a spokesman for the physical and whose motto is 'Be a good animal.' But he lives in miserable circumstances and appears to treat his wife as no more than a convenience for breeding. At the end of the narrative, George, another representative of physical life, is in a bad way. It is a paradox of much of Lawrence's writing that, although he appears to be insisting on the superiority of life in the body to life in the mind, those who take the bodily route tend to be no less unfortunate than those who don't.

Lawrence quickly made friends in Croydon, both with colleagues at his own school and in the local teaching community. Among the latter was a woman a few years older than himself called Helen Corke, whose major preoccupation was with music. A talented amateur violinist, she invited Lawrence to musical soirées where she herself might play, and if she was not the one to first introduce him to the world of Wagnerian opera, she certainly deepened his understanding of it. He had always been fond of music and at home liked nothing better than a sing-song around a piano, which first his mother and later his younger sister, Ada, would play. But this was music at a different level and must have strengthened that sense of in-betweenness to which he refers in 'Red-herring'.

In spite of the exciting new life he was living in Croydon, Lawrence's links with home remained strong. Along with Keats and Byron, he is one of the greatest of all letter writers in English literature, and anyone who reads through the eight volumes of his collected correspondence can gather a strong and vivid sense of what kind of person he was. Yet the letters he wrote to his mother from Croydon every week have all disappeared, as a result of which any account of his youth will always be partial. In August 1909, when he was almost 24, he took part in the annual family holiday with his parents. This was more adventurous than usual in that it took them to the Isle of Wight, rather than to Skegness or Mablethorpe. He learned later that, by a strange coincidence, Corke had been on the island at the same time, spending a week with a man who was her violin teacher. A professional musician, he had a wife back in London, as well as several children. When he returned home, the impossibility of his domestic situation appears to have combined with a depressive temperament and driven him to hang himself. Corke became friendly enough with Lawrence to show him some of the writing in which she had tried to come to terms with this traumatic event, and they agreed that he should use what she had written as a basis for what would turn out to be his second novel, *The Trespasser*.

The Isle of Wight holiday would be the last of its kind for Lawrence and his family since, in the August of the following year (1910), his mother fell seriously ill of what proved to be an incurable cancer when she was visiting relatives in Leicester. A young woman called Louie Burrows, whom Lawrence had known and liked at college, happened to have a teaching post in the area at that time and was helpful to him in getting his mother seen by doctors and then transported back to Eastwood, where she died on 9 December 1910. Lydia Lawrence had remained the centre of her youngest son's world, despite all his new experiences, so the effect on him was catastrophic. Often on compassionate leave from his job in Croydon, he played a large part in caring for her while she was dying and, in the process, saw a lot of Louie Burrows. A week before Lydia's death, he had been on a train with Louie when he impulsively proposed to her and was accepted. It may be that as he saw the guiding light of his existence about to be extinguished, he was desperate to find another. When he told his mother what he had done, she was hesitant at first but then approved – as she certainly would not have done had her son told her that he planned to marry Jessie Chambers, whom she quite positively disliked.

Lawrence's engagement to Louie Burrows at the end of 1910 may have helped to address some of the emotional problems associated with his mother's death, but it did nothing to ease his sexual frustration. One of the closest male friends of his youth was a man called George Neville. He later recorded how Lawrence had once told him that he wanted to write about sex but to go much deeper than any novelist had ever gone before. This was because it was 'the most important thing in our existence' and 'the only thing worth writing about'.[7] Neville clearly found this remark strange, given that it was made at a time when sex was a matter which his friend knew very little about. But if in his early writing days Lawrence's personal experience did not allow him to write authoritatively about sexual intercourse, it did not prevent him from being an expert on sexual frustration, and there are powerful descriptions in his writing of what this feels like from the male point of view.

It seems likely that Alice Dax, the unusually libertarian and feminist wife of an Eastwood chemist, slept with Lawrence at least once, and he may have used sex workers very occasionally, but what he was desperate to find was a regular sexual partner among the young women he knew. Only the force of his pent-up feelings can explain, although not excuse, the decision he had made at the end of 1909 to ask Jessie Chambers to have sex with him. It is clear from all he wrote about her in various thinly disguised forms that, although he was very close to Jessie in intellectual and spiritual terms, he did not find her physically attractive, or at least had developed over the years the habit of thinking of her more like a sister than a girlfriend. Asking her to sleep with him, with only vague assurances of a future marriage, was to exploit cruelly his knowledge of her devotion to his wellbeing. On the few occasions they had sex she offered herself up in a spirit of self-sacrifice, which seems to have contributed to his disappointment with the experience and led to his decision that the two of them could have no future together (the whole episode would be dramatized in *Sons and Lovers*, in the chapter with the shamefully unfair title of 'The Test on Miriam').

Lawrence did find Louie Burrows physically attractive, which was a major reason for his proposing to her, but though she no doubt loved him she was not devoted in Jessie's fashion, and in any case had very firm religious principles. Lawrence had abandoned his Christian faith a few years before, largely because he found it impossible to reconcile the idea of a benevolent and omnipotent God with the degree of unmerited suffering in the world. Burrows, however, was a stout Anglican and resisted firmly all the attempts he made to anticipate their wedding.

They had agreed that this could only take place when he had saved £100, enough for them to set up house in an area where, initially at least, they would both carry on teaching. This does not now seem a large sum, but it was the equivalent of his annual salary, and both were no doubt thinking of the extra money he could earn from his writing. After all, *The White Peacock*, an advance copy of which he was able to place in his mother's hands a few days before her death, had brought him £50 ('£50!', his father had exclaimed, 'an' tha's niver done a day's hard work in thy life').[8] Two more works along these lines and he would be in a position to marry, especially given the payments he received for the poems or short stories he occasionally published, although these fees were of course much lower (he never had much luck with his plays). Yet prolific though he was, Lawrence was neither a writing machine nor naturally overflowing with subjects outside his personal experience: the stories and sketches he wrote were mostly based on real incidents from the working-class mining life he knew, episodes that had occurred at his school or the complexities of his own love life. This difficulty, coupled with the need he now felt to make money, helps to explain why he worked hard at *The Trespasser*, the novel which relied for its starting point on what Corke had already written about those days on the Isle of Wight immediately preceding the suicide of her lover.

Corke had provided Lawrence with a situation, the short holiday spent with her violin teacher on the Isle of Wight, and the latter's suicide had given him a dramatic conclusion. Rather than adding any new incidents, he chose to bear down on these two crucial elements. The most impressive part of *The Trespasser* comes with the relatively brief account of the return of Siegmund (as the violin teacher is called) to his home in suburban London and the understandably hostile reception he receives there from his wife and children. The hopelessness he feels in being unable to progress in his career, and too burdened with family responsibilities ever to be able to make a new life with Helena, are described in ways that make his decision to take his own life comprehensible. There are also, of course, powerful passages in the much longer preceding section describing his time on the Isle of Wight with 'Helena', but although there are a couple of obscure indications that she does in fact sleep with him, the effect is curiously more one of sexual frustration than satisfaction. This may well be because, in order to make Siegmund come alive as a character, Lawrence projected onto him much of his own relations with Corke.

It is clear that, despite his engagement to Louie, Lawrence tried hard to persuade Corke to have sex with him. In Chapter Fourteen of *Lady Chatterley's Lover*, Mellors offers Connie a review of his previous girlfriends. He describes the first as 'the romantic sort that hated commonness', who 'egged me on to poetry and reading' so that 'we were the most literary cultured couple in ten counties'. But 'the serpent in the grass was sex', which he claims this girl did not have, 'at least, not where it is supposed to be'. He admits that he was the one who talked her into their sleeping together and that the outcome was so unsuccessful that 'I was cruel, and left her.' The references to Jessie Chambers here seem unmistakable, but equally explicit are those in Mellor's account of the second girl he took up with, since she is described as a teacher who played the fiddle and 'had made a scandal by carrying on with a married man and driving him nearly out of his mind'. According to him, this Corke figure was 'a demon':

> She loved everything about love, except the sex. Clinging, caressing, creeping into you in every way: but if you forced her to the sex itself, she just ground her teeth and sent out hate. I forced her to it, and she could simply numb me with hate because of it.[9]

It would seem from this that Lawrence did have sex with Corke, but what is evident from more contemporary accounts is that he certainly tried to, in spite of his commitments elsewhere.

Lawrence always had difficulty with titles for his novels: a peacock does appear in *The White Peacock*, but it is hardly central to the action, and it is not at all clear who is doing the trespassing in *The Trespasser*. For the third novel, on which he had now embarked, he initially chose the more straightforward solution of titling the work by the central character's name: Paul Morel. When Lawrence showed an early version to Jessie Chambers, she inadvertently heaped coals of fire on her own head by suggesting that it should be more autobiographical than it already was, which made the parts involving her even more painfully damaging. It must have been very hard for Jessie, after she had become a schoolteacher in the provinces, to accept the ease with which anyone at all familiar with her circumstances could discover from *Sons and Lovers* (as 'Paul Morel' became) that she had slept with its author. Lawrence was ruthless in using his own personal experience in his fiction, and the problem of having great writers portray you is that there is no effective comeback to whatever you may legitimately perceive as inaccurate or unfair.

Lawrence's correspondence with Louie suggests that she nagged him to get on with 'Paul Morel', knowing the importance of the money it would bring to their future, but he was not always in the mood and was distracted by new acquaintances and experiences, as well as by the daily grind of his school teaching. He must have already been thinking of abandoning the profession and trying to survive as a writer, but although that may have seemed possible while he remained single, it must have looked far more difficult should his marriage go ahead. The people he had met through Hueffer were an encouragement for him to think of a writing career, and one of these was Edward Garnett, a minor author and advisor to several publishers. A strong advocate for Lawrence's work, Garnett was another of his many new acquaintances with views on sexual morality that differed considerably from those back in the Midlands. He lived in a large imitation-fifteenth-century cottage called The Cearne, which he had had built on a beautiful patch of countryside in Hampshire. In November 1911, returning from a visit there, Lawrence was caught in the rain. Back in Croydon, a cold quickly developed into pneumonia, and he became gravely ill.

At first, Lawrence only wanted his sister Ada to look after him, in addition to a local nurse, but he was happy enough to see Louie once the crisis was past. In January 1912, he spent almost a month of convalescence in Bournemouth and then a week at The Cearne. Times when people think they might well have died often provoke re-evaluation, and it was during his convalescence that Lawrence resigned his post at his school and also wrote to Louie breaking off their engagement. He was helped in this painful task by one of his doctors having said that, if ever he went back to school teaching, he would be threatened with TB (although the test he had for that disease during his illness had proved negative). With the idyll of teaching with Louie in some country school gone, all he now had to provide for was himself.

2
Turning Point

Once he had abandoned teaching, it must have seemed to Lawrence that he needed some kind of occupation to fall back on, given the uncertainties of a writer's life, so he thought of spending some time in Germany in order to become more qualified for private tutoring work at home. He was presumably confident that, as a language tutor in England, he could teach French, and his interest in German had been stimulated by Corke as well as by the fact that one of his mother's sisters had married a German. This uncle by marriage had family connections back in Germany, which meant that Lawrence would not be going there knowing nobody at all. He nevertheless felt it would be useful to have some further contacts, so he dropped a note to his former professor of languages at Nottingham, Ernest Weekley, asking for help. Weekley invited Lawrence to lunch at his house on 17 March 1912, in one of the city's leafier suburbs. There, Lawrence was initially entertained by Weekley's German wife, Frieda. Biographers are inclined to talk too easily of turning points, which are often more important for the structure of their narratives than their subjects' fortunes, but this was a meeting that certainly changed Lawrence's life for ever.

There are several reasons why Lawrence should have been so impressed by Frieda Weekley that, after only a few days, he was describing her as the most wonderful woman in England and wondering how he could spend the rest of his life with her – even though she was five and a half years older than he was, the mother of three children, and someone else's wife. Photographs of the time show her to have been attractive – 'awfully good-looking', in

Frieda Lawrence as a young woman.

Lawrence's own words – and she was also highly articulate and full of ideas.[1] All his previous girlfriends had been readers and aware of much current thinking on matters such as religion or women's suffrage, but Frieda had the advantage over them of being in touch with an intellectual avant-garde. She had made annual trips to Germany, where her elder sister was married to a professor of economics called Edgar Jaffé. This couple were part of a group that included Otto Gross, one of several men with whom Frieda had previously had an affair. Gross was an enthusiastic disciple of Sigmund Freud and had come to the conclusion that, since so many of the psychological difficulties Freud analysed could be traced back to sexual frustration, the most effective treatment would be free love. Freud, aware of how damaging this solution would be to the discipline he was struggling to establish, especially if the analysts themselves began sleeping with their patients, eventually expelled Gross from the psychoanalytic community – but not before Frieda had thoroughly imbibed his point of view. It follows that one of her several attractions for Lawrence was that she was ready to sleep with him almost immediately, and it did not lessen her appeal that she was not only foreign but a foreign aristocrat. Her family name was von Richthofen, and one of her distant cousins would later become notorious in England as an enemy fighter pilot known as 'the Red Baron'.

It was a great help to the lovers that, in the weeks after Lawrence and Frieda met, she could begin preparing her annual German visit. This meant that on 3 May 1912 they could travel together to the border town of Metz, where her father was a member of the military administration (his injuries having forced him to give up more active army service). At first, Frieda tried to hide Lawrence's presence from most of her family, and when that became impossible she encouraged him to retreat north, to a village not far from Cologne, where his aunt's relations lived. A struggle between him and Frieda then went on at a distance, she having begun by thinking of her relationship with Lawrence as just another affair, while he wanted nothing less than full commitment. As soon as 8 May, he had written a letter to Weekley in which he declared, 'I love your wife and she loves me,' explaining that 'Mrs Weekley is afraid of being stunted and not allowed to grow, and so she must live her own life.' 'To me,' he added, 'it means the future. I feel as if my effort of life was all for her.'[2] It seems that Lawrence gave this letter to Frieda to post, which after much hesitation she did, although she must have had at least some inkling of how difficult her life might become, separated from her children and without any income of her own.

It may be that Frieda thought her husband would never deny her access to her children or even that he would be 'gentlemanly' enough to provide her with some money, yet the decision she made to stay with Lawrence, against the advice of her family, nevertheless appears from this distance in time either a very brave or a very foolhardy one. But she was in love – and, besides, she soon came to regard Lawrence in the light of her mission. All his previous girlfriends were 'feminist' to a greater or lesser extent, although only Alice Dax appears to have extended the feminist belief in more freedom for women into the sexual field. But Frieda had taken from her avant-garde German contacts the idea that it was the destiny of women to release the creative powers in troubled young men, especially if they happened to be geniuses (and it was in those terms that her husband, perhaps half jokingly, had already talked about Lawrence). Anyone who drew from this the conclusion that she was thereby condemning herself to a subsidiary handmaiden role would not have known her well. She was delighted to observe how effortlessly Lawrence could write, whatever his material circumstances. He is 'joy in *all* moods', she wrote on 21 May to Garnett, whom Lawrence had taken her to meet shortly before they left England, 'and it is fearfully exciting when he writes and I watch while it comes and it is a thrill'.[3] But she could fiercely criticize what he produced, as well as what she considered to be the unhealthy mental states from which the words sometimes emanated. She was fond of claiming that she was more or less the co-author of novels like *Sons and Lovers* and *The Rainbow*, partly on the grounds that Lawrence was an emotional wreck before their first meeting, and it was only through her that his real talent had been released. She also pointed out that she had talked to him often about what women felt and had even herself written various parts in the novels where women figured. Whatever the insecurities of life with him, it must have seemed preferable to carrying on her comfortable existence in a Nottingham suburb.

For Lawrence himself, continuing to write became much more of a necessity now there were two mouths to feed rather than just one. With their author's preternatural alertness to the natural environment, his letters show how powerful an impact new sights and sounds had on him as he and Frieda, borrowing houses and living as economically as possible, moved to an area below Munich, in sight of the Alps. The sketches he wrote as they made these moves mark the beginning of his career as a travel writer. The publication of several of them, partly through the informal agency of Garnett, brought in some money, as did the published appearance in England or America of an occasional short story or poem. But it was on 'Paul Morel' that he was chiefly relying to carry them through the winter. It was a major blow when, in July, Heinemann wrote to say that, having now read the novel, he had decided that 'its want of reticence' would mean that it would almost certainly be refused by the circulating libraries, and that he therefore could not publish it.[4] Fortunately, Garnett almost immediately came to Lawrence's rescue by finding another firm, Duckworth, who agreed to publish the book after a revision which Garnett oversaw himself. This brought in £100, half of which Lawrence received after he and Frieda had crossed the Alps and settled in a small Italian village called Gargnano on the shores of Lake Garda.

To save money, as well as for the experience, they had decided to make some of the journey across the Bavarian Alps, into Austria and then Italy, on foot. While still in the mountains, they were joined at one point by Garnett's son David, known as 'Bunny', to whom

Gargnano, Italy.

they were anxious to be as helpful as possible given all his father was doing for Lawrence. Bunny Garnett was studying botany in London, and he arrived with another student called Hobson. After the students had left, and at a particularly fraught moment when the couple seemed to have lost their way in the mountains, Frieda told Lawrence that she had had sex with Hobson, as if to remind him that he was not the only young man to whom her healing powers were available. Her attitude to sex had been a liberation for him, but the hard lesson he was forced to learn was that there was no guarantee of it operating exclusively in his favour.

The area in which the couple settled was beautiful, full of stimuli for the eye, and Lawrence embraced the challenge it presented for him to work out the differences between local Italians and the people he knew at home and incorporate the results in more travel sketches. His major preoccupation since receiving Heinemann's letter, however, had been the revision of what had now become *Sons and Lovers*, in an indication of Frieda's influence. One way that influence operated is apparent from a synopsis of the novel that Lawrence sent to Garnett from Italy in November 1912. In it he talks of how, as her sons grow up, Mrs Morel 'selects them as lovers' so that, when they come to manhood, they can't love, 'because their mother is the strongest power in their lives . . . As soon as the young men come into contact with women, there's a split.' It is this split which is responsible for the death of Paul Morel's older brother, William, but then Paul 'decides to leave his soul in his mother's hands, and like his elder brother, go for passion':

> He gets passion. Then the split begins to tell again. But, almost unconsciously, the mother realizes what is the matter, and begins to die. The son casts off his mistress, attends to his mother dying. He is left in the end naked of everything with the drift towards death.[5]

One of the criticisms made of Lawrence's previous novels was their relative formlessness. Here he was at least giving *Sons and Lovers* a unifying theme and justifying its new title.

It is fortunate that Lawrence's third novel was not in fact anywhere near as crudely programmatic as he made it seem in his synopsis. Some of the scenes in which Paul comes home to his mother, after seeing Miriam (the character based on Jessie Chambers), have a sexual element that may have been added in response to Frieda's analysis of what Lawrence's relation to his mother had been, but the bulk of the early part of the novel remains true to Jessie's injunction that it should stick as closely as possible to his past life. The return of the body of Lawrence's elder brother, called William in the novel, now made a highly effective scene, as did Mrs Morel's earlier stout defence of William against a neighbour who accused him of tearing her own son's collar. There is matchless ease in the descriptions of Mr Morel getting up early to make his own breakfast, talking with the children about his favourite pit pony or making fuses for blowing coal down from the coalface, and great tenderness in the account of Mrs Morel bargaining with a man at the local market for a small decorative pot to brighten her living room, or taking Paul out to tea in Nottingham after he has secured a job in a surgical-goods factory. The skill in this second episode is impressive as Lawrence describes how Paul's mother deals as best she can with a waitress who indicates in her disdainful manner that this small, neat woman, accompanied by a desperately embarrassed adolescent, is not at all used to spending money in cafés. The first part of *Sons and Lovers* is packed with scenes from a particular kind of working-class life which had never been so well described, and never will be again, since the conditions that gave rise to them no longer exist. Writers tend not to value sufficiently what comes relatively easily to them, and there was one point in the long revision process of *Sons and Lovers* when Lawrence talked of shortening the novel by cutting out some of its childhood parts. After it was published, he said he would never write like that again. One can only be thankful that he did, and that his own particular brand of social realism was a mode which always remained available to him.

    In the second part of *Sons and Lovers*, which deals with Paul Morel's love life, Frieda's input into the descriptions of his affair with Clara Dawes, a married woman who is separated from her husband, was no doubt considerable. In Chapter Twelve, finally called 'Passion', Lawrence dwells impressively on the intensity of Paul's needs and feelings, even if he sometimes seems to have a greater interest in them than most readers could ever feel. Towards the chapter's end there is a brilliantly written episode in which Paul, having missed his train back from Nottingham, spends the night with Clara in the house of her suspicious but strangely complicit mother. A peculiarity of Lawrence's treatment of the whole situation with Clara is the way Paul's attitude to her husband, Baxter Dawes, is slowly transformed from dislike and hostility into sympathy, so that, at the end, he seems more comfortable in Baxter's company than his wife's. It would be hard to say how much Lawrence was thinking of Ernest Weekley as he put the final touches to his revision of *Sons and Lovers* and then, meekly if reluctantly, submitted to the changes Garnett felt had to be made to prevent Duckworths from reacting in the way Heinemann had. As he said at the time, he now simply could not afford for the novel to remain unpublished and himself unpaid.

At the end of *Sons and Lovers*, Paul Morel and Baxter Dawes are reconciled, and Clara returns to her husband. By contrast, Weekley's relations with his wife and her lover went from bad to worse. In the early weeks after Frieda had left, there was an epistolary discussion of some kind of compromise, which would almost certainly have meant her giving up Lawrence, but soon Weekley's attitude hardened, and he determined to divorce Frieda (the letter Lawrence had written to him would be used by his lawyers in the divorce proceedings and published in a Nottingham newspaper). The major bone of contention would be the children to whom Weekley was trying to deny Frieda access. This was extremely painful for her, and her concern over them became a continuing source of problems in her relationship with Lawrence, who was inclined to feel that, having once made her choice, she should be prepared to stick by its consequences. Their first months together were largely idyllic, each of them adapting well to a bohemian lifestyle in what were usually beautiful surroundings, and able to forget about their financial problems. But as time went on, they often quarrelled violently, in part because they had both accepted Otto Gross's belief in the evil of restraint (it was because she had always to exercise self-restraint, Lawrence came to feel, that his mother had allowed cancer to get the better of her). They became so used to letting fly that they continued to do so when other people were present, and the violence of their quarrels shocked their friends to the point where it seemed impossible that they could stay together. But through his close relation to his mother, Lawrence had developed an emotional dependency which he struggled hard to overcome. Frieda did not have that problem, but she had burnt her boats in leaving Weekley and, were she to leave Lawrence, would hardly have had anywhere else she could easily go, especially once war had broken out and a retreat to her family was no longer feasible.

In June 1913, Lawrence and Frieda returned to England for a short time. By that date, *Sons and Lovers* had been published, to largely favourable reviews if only moderate commercial success. From London they retreated to a rented flat in Kingsgate on the North Kent coast, where they were visited by the writer and civil servant Eddie Marsh. He had included a poem by Lawrence in an anthology called *Georgian Poetry* (after the George who happened to be on the British throne at the time) and was well connected in government circles. Marsh introduced Lawrence and Frieda to Herbert Asquith, the son of the prime minister, and his aristocratic wife, Lady Cynthia, who were also staying in Kingsgate at that period. It pleased Frieda to be moving in social circles roughly analogous to some of those she had known as a young woman, and it appears to have gratified Lawrence also, even though his mother was no longer alive to observe how well he had 'got on'. But both of them enjoyed as much, if not more, the company of another couple they met for the first time during this period: John Middleton Murry and his New Zealand partner, Katherine Mansfield. They had previously written to Lawrence asking him to contribute to a short-lived literary review they had launched, and what helped to bring the two couples together was that each was as short of money as the other. A further binding factor was that Murry and Mansfield were not yet married. It worried Lawrence that in socializing with people

Lady Cynthia Mary Evelyn Asquith (née Charteris), 16 April 1912.

like the Asquiths he might be thought to be doing so under false pretences, since they were unlikely to be aware of the real situation.

Frieda had wanted to come to England partly to seek legal advice about her divorce, while for Lawrence there was the wedding of his sister Ada, which he had promised to attend. But by August they were back in Germany and contemplating another prolonged stay in Italy, not this time on Lake Garda but near the Gulf of La Spezia. Edgar Jaffé had been staying nearby, which may have been significant, but it was of course an area Lawrence would already have known about as the last place where Percy Bysshe Shelley had lived before he drowned, and where Lord Byron and a few other friends had cremated that poet's remains. Along the coastline, not far from where the cremation had taken place, in an isolated bay called Fiascherino, Lawrence and Frieda found a house which struck them as ideal and where he could settle down to work.

His problem was how to follow up *Sons and Lovers* with another novel. There had been several false starts. He thought at one point of writing one based around the life of Robert Burns, who had always interested him, but transposed to the Midlands. He did a good deal of writing on a novel about the difficulties for women of breaking away from a provincial background which, much later, would become *The Lost Girl*, but most of his energies went on a work initially called 'The Sisters'. It is in this that prototypes of Ursula and Gudrun Brangwen first appear, but it would be some time before they would develop into the protagonists of *The Rainbow* and *Women in Love*. He was the kind of writer who would discover what he needed to write as he wrote, and then go back to write a fresh version which would nevertheless incorporate much of the original material.

In its different way, Fiascherino was as idyllic as Gargnano had been, but neither Frieda nor Lawrence was hermit-like in temperament, and at first they suffered from isolation. Yet they soon became close enough to the locals to be invited to a wedding; some poetry-writing friends of Eddie Marsh dropped in to see them (as would Eddie Marsh himself later); and through those contacts they were introduced to a number of wealthy expatriates living in the area and found themselves invited to dinner or tea in their palatial residences. One of several other visitors was especially important. When she had read *Sons and Lovers,* Ivy Low, who had herself already published two novels, had sent postcards to all her friends proclaiming its Freudian merits. 'Discovered a genius,' these said. 'Be sure to read *Sons and Lovers*. This is a book about the Oedipus complex.'[6] Low had an aunt called Barbara, who was one of the first psychoanalysts in Britain, and it was through the two of them that Lawrence would later come to know several other early practitioners in the psychoanalytic movement. Low stayed with the Lawrences for all of six weeks, which was too long, especially for Frieda, who now had her first experience of dealing with women who regarded her husband with something close to awe.

The two lovers were waiting for the period after Frieda's divorce when the decree nisi would become absolute, so that they could then go to England and get married. They left Italy in June 1914, and their wedding took place in the Kensington Registry Office on the thirteenth of the following month. In the period just before, Lawrence had been in communication with one of London's leading literary agents, J. B. Pinker (Henry James and Joseph Conrad were two of the writers he represented). Impressed by *Sons and Lovers*, Pinker had suggested that he could get Lawrence an advance of £300 for his next novel. For someone always worrying about where the next few pounds would come from, this was a very large sum, but accepting Pinker's offer would mean deserting Duckworths, who had helped him out when he was in trouble. Not feeling he was in a position to refuse £300, Lawrence attempted to compensate Duckworths by offering them a volume of his short stories.

Wedding photograph of the Lawrences, with John Middleton Murry and Katherine Mansfield in attendance.

This collection appeared in October 1914 and contained twelve stories dating from his earliest beginnings as a writer until very recent times. All but one had been published before, although several were extensively revised before the volume appeared. The exception was first called 'Two Marriages' and then 'The Daughters of the Vicar', and it had remained unpublished because it was too long, more than twice or three times the average length of the others. At almost 19,000 words, it was in fact not a short story at all, but the first of Lawrence's novellas, of which he would write half a dozen more during his career. If he had produced nothing else, these works alone would have qualified him as one of the twentieth century's greatest writers.

The narrative of 'The Daughters of the Vicar' is relatively straightforward. An Anglican clergyman and his wife find themselves marooned in a mining community in the Midlands, with the result that their daughters have very little opportunity for meeting suitable marriage partners. The whole family is excited when they learn that they are to be sent a new curate but they are disappointed when he arrives, because, although he has the requisite private income, he turns out to be physically underdeveloped – 'a little abortion' is how the embittered vicar's wife cruelly describes him.[7] The elder daughter, carefully weighing up all her options, and prompted by the charitable feelings Christianity enjoins, decides to accept this man's eventual proposal of marriage. Meanwhile, the younger daughter has become physically attracted to a young miner and in time opts for marrying him. This outrages her parents, who are relieved when they learn that these two young people will emigrate and save them having to endure the social embarrassment to which they feel such an unsuitable marriage would inevitably give rise.

The vicar represents a dilemma for the Anglican church, which Lawrence conveys with considerable sociological acuity. Its old parishes, with their often beautiful buildings, were becoming overrun with a new industrial population which had none of the traditional respect or reverence for the established church and had either turned to Nonconformism or become more or less pagan.

The vicar's wife resents these changes even more than her husband and is represented by Lawrence with impressive satirical edge. One can imagine that his descriptions of family life at the vicarage are what Jane Austen might have written, had she been living a hundred years later and adapting to changed social circumstances. Very unlike an Austen of whatever period, however, is the way Lawrence deals with the physical disabilities of the curate. These fill the vicar's wife less with pity than with an instinctive disgust, and one can sense the influence of Friedrich Nietzsche, whom Lawrence seems to have read, in the way they are presented as the inevitable origin of the curate's cold character, of a spirituality essentially heartless. It is a chilling portrait which makes the older sister's decision to marry him appear all the more fundamentally immoral. But that the decision the younger sister takes could not be dismissed as 'romantic' is evident from how Lawrence makes his reader aware of the difficulties she has in adapting to married life with someone whose class background is so different from her own.

The strength of 'The Daughters of the Vicar' derives from Lawrence's deep knowledge of the provincial English environment in which he grew up, but the other outstanding story in the collection shows how quickly he would feel his way into a culture previously foreign to him. 'The Prussian Officer' was composed while he was still abroad, and in June 1913 he described it as the best short story he had ever written.[8] If it could be said to have had a major source, it is in Frieda's talk of having grown up in a garrison town where there were lots of soldiers around, and perhaps also in Lawrence's own time in Metz and meeting with Frieda's father. The story is essentially a case study; one key to understanding it is the remark Lawrence had made to Garnett in November 1912 that 'sex lust fermented makes atrocity'.[9]

It would be too simple to say that the story is only about the dangers of repressed homosexuality. A Prussian officer who has spent a lifetime exercising severe self-restraint is irritated by his orderly's apparent lack of self-consciousness and by the easy naturalness with which he moves about. At the same time, he clearly finds him physically attractive. The orderly, for his part, is concerned not to establish any kind of genuine rapport with the officer and, since he is not an enlisted man, only anxious to get through his last three months of compulsory service so that he can go home. Increasingly keen to elicit some kind of response from the young man, the officer is reduced to deriving what perverse pleasure he can from kicking him after he has refused to explain why he has a pencil behind his ear (he had been using it to write to his girlfriend). The orderly's body is still aching from this treatment when he has to follow the officer on manoeuvres. The landscape in which these take place is described with Lawrence's habitual expertise, but for the most part readers are entirely in the heads of the two protagonists as the tension between them builds. This eventually reaches such a pitch that the orderly attacks the officer, who gets his spur caught in a tree root and falls on his back:

> In a second the orderly, with serious, earnest young face, and underlip between his teeth, had got his knee in the officer's chest and was pressing the chin backward over the farther edge of the tree-stump, pressing, with all his heart behind in a passion of relief, the tension of his wrists exquisite with relief... He did not relax one hair's-breadth, but, all the force of all his blood exulting in his thrust, he shoved back the head of the other man, till there was a little 'cluck' and a crunching sensation.[10]

In destroying the officer, the orderly knows he has also destroyed himself, and he rides off to his death in the woods. What is both remarkable and original in the story is the way Lawrence finds methods for describing the unspoken feelings of his two men, who actually *say* very little to each other. The result makes for absorbing reading, although it also indicates how far Lawrence could be from regarding literature as mere entertainment.

3

The Rainbow

The Lawrences cannot have been the only couple whose more immediate plans were thrown into disarray by the outbreak of war between Great Britain and Germany on 4 August 1914. What it meant in their case was that a visit which they had intended to last only a few months was extended over several years. One problem of living in England for someone like Lawrence was the climate – he would spend many days of every English winter in bed with a bad cold, flu or bronchitis – but another was the expense (he and Frieda had been able to live much more cheaply in Italy). A new friend they made on their return to England was Gilbert Cannan, a successful novelist who was living with his wife Mary in a converted mill-house near the village of Chesham in Buckinghamshire. It was he who alerted the Lawrences to a cottage in the area which could be rented very cheaply, and into which they moved in mid-August, after the period in London that had followed their marriage in July. The Cannans frequently entertained friends from the literary and artistic world, to whom the Lawrences would be introduced, including the rising young writer Compton Mackenzie and his wife, and they acquired more regular company when Murry and Mansfield came to live in another cottage nearby.

It was partly because of Cannan that, in October, Lawrence received £50 from the Royal Society of Literature, a gift or handout for struggling authors which excited in him a complicated mixture of gratitude, relief, anger and resentment. His main source of income now consisted in whatever was left of the advance of £135 he had received from the publisher Methuen & Co. and any smaller sums Pinker was willing to advance him in anticipation of another £135 that would be due once the novel – which had begun as *The Sisters*, had become *The Wedding Ring* and was now being revised into *The Rainbow* – was finally published (the sums were minus his agent's 10 per cent).

If his life was becoming increasingly difficult, it was also in part because, now she was back in England, Frieda was intent on seeing her children. Her impulsive nature led to her making an unannounced and unauthorized visit to the house in Chiswick where the children were living with their grandparents and, later, bursting in on her ex-husband while he was in Nottingham. The effect was only to harden his resolve, and he took additional legal measures to keep her at arm's length. Her unhappiness took a heavy toll on her relationship with Lawrence and was one of the many factors behind their frequent quarrels. Continuing anxiety about money did not help, and neither did illness. It was on one of the occasions when he was laid low with a fluey cold that Lawrence grew the beard with which he was afterwards always associated.

The continuing war was increasingly intolerable to him, especially as he had a wife who, behind her back, was occasionally referred to by some of his friends as 'the Hun'. His problems strengthened a tendency he had always had to 'philosophize', to find some satisfactory intellectual context that would allow him to make sense of what was happening, both to him and the world at large. In 1913 he had written a foreword to *Sons and Lovers* (which was really an afterword), in the opening to which he indicated what would become a major theme of his more philosophical thinking. 'John, the beloved disciple,' he began, 'says "The Word was made Flesh." But why should he turn things around? The women simply go on bearing talkative sons, as an answer. "The Flesh was made Word."'[1] This witty reversal of the biblical order settles the competing claims of body and mind by insisting that body must always come first. It can be associated with a famous letter Lawrence had sent to Ernest Collings on 17 January 1913, in which he writes, 'My great religion is a belief in the blood, the flesh, as being wiser than the intellect. We can go wrong in our minds. But what our blood feels and believes, and says, is always true.' In 1914 Lawrence seized the opportunity of an offer he had received to write a book on Thomas Hardy, to develop his thinking. The resulting work became more a question of his own speculations than criticism of its subject's novels (although there is some of that).

Lawrence's two opposing principles of body and mind appear under many different guises in his *Study of Thomas Hardy*, including as God the Father and God the Son or, more simply even if more enigmatically, Law and Love. The results are sometimes paradoxical. God the Father, for example, turns out to represent a female principle (in the opening to the *Sons and Lovers* foreword, Lawrence is reminding us that it is women who bear the babies), while the person he thinks of as best representing the masculinity of God the Son is Shelley, although this is largely on account of the poem 'To a Skylark', with its references to disembodied beauty ('Bird thou never wert'). The meaning of 'flesh' remains reasonably constant for Lawrence, but apart from intellect and mind, 'word' also takes on ideas of spirituality, hence its link with God the Son, who is associated with the belief that we should love others more than we love ourselves.

It would take a complete book, and one much longer than this, to describe what Lawrence's philosophy finally amounted to. This is partly because it kept being rewritten, went off in all directions and never became entirely coherent (or if it did, it was in texts that have not survived). But one of its important and recurrent features was that it showed him habitually viewing the world through a series of antinomies. Critics have traced the influence of this dualistic style of thinking, as well as that of his having recently re-read much of Hardy's fiction, on *The Rainbow*. From those prototypes in *The Sisters* of both Ursula and Gudrun Brangwen, as well as of Gerald Crich and Rupert Birkin, Lawrence had proceeded backwards into establishing an appropriate background for Ursula in both her parents and then, finally, her grandparents. In the opening he wrote for *The Rainbow*, full of biblical language and imagery, Lawrence evokes the rural setting in which her grandfather, Tom Brangwen, grows up – an environment governed by tradition and instinct. Some stirrings of dissatisfaction are suggested by the way Tom appears driven to court and marry not a local English girl but the Polish widow who is serving as a housekeeper for the vicar. In general, however, it is the Brangwen women who are represented as striving towards a different and (in their view) finer life, one in which there is more contact with new ideas and the outside world and less subservience to age-long practices and the rhythm of the seasons. It is they who are under the influence of God the Son rather than his father, of love rather than law.

The vicar's Polish housekeeper brings to her marriage with Tom a young daughter by a previous husband. Her child, Anna, will go on to marry her cousin (by law if not blood) Will Brangwen and become the mother of Ursula. She is the person who will finally break out of the Brangwen enclosure and, as an elementary-school teacher, take her place with some difficulty in what Lawrence describes as the 'man's world'. One theme of *The Rainbow* is therefore a very ambitious one: nothing less than the charting through a representative family of the transition in England from a rural to an industrial society (a process much accelerated in that mid-nineteenth century in which *The Rainbow* begins). What Lawrence sets out to represent is the difference this change made to individuals, particularly when they happened to be female. By the time he had reached Ursula's entry into the modern world of work, he had realized that he had more than enough on his hands for a single novel and decided to reserve all the other material from *The Sisters* for a sequel to *The Rainbow*, which only later would be called *Women in Love*.

Readers of *Sons and Lovers* who knew something of his origins could well have concluded that he was essentially an autobiographical writer, unlikely to do his best work when he moved away from personal experience. There are moments in *The Rainbow* that relate directly to Lawrence's own life – his highly effective descriptions of Ursula's first months as a teacher or college student would be among them – but mostly there is in this novel a breadth of imagination that takes him well beyond personal reminiscence. Nothing, of course, ever comes from nothing; in describing the farm environment in which Tom Brangwen grows up, as well as the early married life of Ursula's parents, Will and Anna, he seems to have been helped by what Louie Burrows had told him about her forbears. She and Jessie Chambers were no doubt unacknowledged and non-consulted contributors to his brilliant account of the romantic tendencies in Ursula's girlhood and adolescence, while he could hardly have dealt with her early sexual experiences without some help from Frieda. But there are other fine passages that are less easily traced back to their origins, even in this partial and rudimentary fashion, and which seem to come from the way a great novelist's imagination can be fed by mere floating fragments of life experience.

After his return to England in August 1914, Lawrence met an astonishing number of significant figures in the literary and political worlds. Most of them seemed to have been powerfully impressed by his conversation, and many by the evidence they saw of his acute psychological insight. He appeared to them to have an uncanny ability to deduce another's feelings and state of mind on relatively slight acquaintance, and from very few indices. What he brings to *The Rainbow*, making it such an original and groundbreaking work, is a whole collection of words and metaphors for applying this insight to fictional characters who are themselves relatively inarticulate. This was the period of Freud's famous 'talking cure', but how do you explore the psychological make-up of someone if they hardly talk? As he had already done in 'The Prussian Officer' and now did much more extensively in *The Rainbow*, Lawrence showed the way in which it was possible to go. A prime example here is the vivid fashion in which he is able to register the alternating waves of intense hatred and love that characterize the early relationship of Will and Anna.

The letters he wrote while he was busy with *The Rainbow* reveal how many of the distinguished and influential friends and acquaintances he now had were strongly attracted to him. His tone in them often approximated to that of an Old Testament prophet or one of the great preachers of the past, and for a while they were as full of Christian terminology and imagery as his novel. But after reading and being very impressed by an academic book about the pre-Socratic Greek philosophers, he changed his tune and decided that Christianity had nothing to offer in the current crisis: 'I am rid of all my Christian religiosity.'[2] These sudden shifts of position were disconcerting and a sign of how volatile he had become as he struggled to find ways of dealing with both his personal problems and those of English society in general.

Adolf de Meyer's portrait of Lady Ottoline Morrell, *c.* 1912, platinum print.

One of the new friends he had made since returning from Fiascherino was Lady Ottoline Morrell, an aristocrat from his own part of the country. She would soon gather around her, principally on an estate recently purchased at Garsington, near Oxford, a group of talented people, all of whom opposed the war. One of these was the mathematician and philosopher Bertrand Russell. It may well have been partly because of Russell that Lawrence began to talk in his letters of the need to nationalize all the country's assets, so that each one of its inhabitants could be freely given an income large enough to live on. This essentially socialist programme was conceived in the context of a greater democracy, yet after espousing it, Lawrence changed his mind on the democratic aspect, telling Russell that letting everyone choose their own government was a mistake: 'Every man should vote according to his understanding, and . . . the highest understanding should dictate for the lower understandings.'[3] This meant that people should only have the power to elect the governing bodies immediately above them, and that there was a need for a system in which aristocrats like Lady Ottoline would retain their position, which would culminate in a dictator as well as a dictatrix responsible for whatever related specifically to women. Not surprisingly, Russell, who had initially been keen on working with Lawrence on anti-war propaganda, found these views unacceptable.

By the time Lawrence was writing his letters to Russell, he had moved from Buckinghamshire to a much more comfortable cottage near Pulborough in West Sussex; it had a bathroom, he would excitedly announce to his friends. When he first came back to England, he had met through Ivy Low a young woman called Catherine Jackson, soon to be Catherine Carswell, and he and Frieda had passed some time with her in Hampstead before moving to Chesham. Another of Ivy's friends with literary ambitions was Viola Meynell, whose father had built on an estate he owned in West Sussex a number of cottages to accommodate his children. Since Viola was not using hers, she was able to offer it to the Lawrences free of charge. They moved there in January 1915 and stayed until August. Many of Lawrence's new friends came to visit them at

The converted barn Viola Meynell lent to the Lawrences is the low building in the foreground.

Greatham, as the village closest to the estate was called, including Russell and E. M. Forster.

It was while he was in the Meynell cottage that Lawrence completed *The Rainbow*. He sent it off at the beginning of March (it would be published in September), and during this period he also wrote a short story called 'England, My England', which relied for many of its background features on the unusual way Viola Meynell's father had organized his family estate. Three of Meynell's daughters, who were clearly in Lawrence's mind as he wrote this story, had their own cottages. Among them was Viola's sister Madeline, who is the model for the character in 'England, My England' called Winifred. Madeline had married Perceval Lucas, who inspired the character named Evelyn in the story's first version (later he is called Egbert). Evelyn has a small private income which is just enough for the couple to survive on, but not when they begin to have children, even though Winifred's father has provided them with free housing. A love marriage which is initially a success begins therefore to break down as Winifred discovers that her husband is not willing to compete in the world in order to make her family financially independent of her father. Matters are brought to a head when one of her daughters has an accident in which she cuts her knee badly. She has to have expensive medical treatment (for which her grandfather pays) but ends up disabled nonetheless. The breakdown in relations between Winifred and Evelyn means that he is all the readier to volunteer for the army when the call comes in 1914 (Perceval Lucas had enlisted at that time, just as the accident to his daughter had indeed taken place).

The difficulty of summarizing the version of 'England, My England' Lawrence initially wrote is that it was radically transformed after the war, and the later version tends to encourage interpretations only hinted at in the earlier one. In 1915, for example, Lawrence's account of a failed marriage was only a brief preliminary sketch, whereas later it became a much-extended psychological portrait of the balance of power in a relationship wherein the husband, handsome and refined though he may be, has neither the force nor enterprise to compete with his wife's father for her loyalty. In this second version, which is one of Lawrence's finest achievements, the fact that Egbert (as Evelyn has become) is *driven* to enlist is made much more obvious. But this difference does not mean that, from the beginning, the Meynell family were not upset that Lawrence should have responded to their hospitality by using them for copy, and they became even more so when, in 1916, Perceval Lucas met the fate the story had in a sense anticipated for him and was killed. The news of his death caused Lawrence to regret that he had ever written 'England, My England' but did not stop his rewritten version containing additional details of the Meynells' arrangements. As Jessie Chambers could have told them, you invited Lawrence into your life at your peril.

During her time at Greatham, Frieda appears to have become highly dissatisfied. Bouts of illness made her husband more irritable than usual, and the periods of intense gloom to which he had always been subject were not shortened by the changes taking place all around him because of the war. She did not get on with Lady Ottoline, who, she felt (with some justification), considered her as altogether too 'earthy' for a man of Lawrence's sensitivity, and

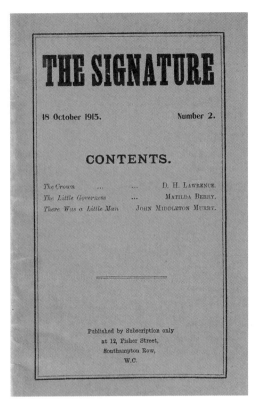

The second issue of *The Signature*, 18 October 1915, containing Lawrence's 'The Crown'.

she often had the feeling that she was regarded by other of his new friends as no more than an annoying appendage. And then there were her children, whom she now had less chance of seeing, buried as she was in the country. She decided that she must go back to London, and the Lawrences found a small flat in Hampstead, where she could go to live away from her husband. This separation, if it could be described as such, did not last long, and by the end of July they were living together in the capital.

In London, Lawrence was reunited with Murry, and together they decided they had to do more to express their opposition to the war and their hopes for the future. With the practical help of a mutual friend called S. S. Koteliansky, who would play an important role in both of their future lives, they hired a room in London where they could hold meetings, and they published by subscription a small magazine entitled *The Signature*. Lawrence's contribution was a series of three essays in which he continued the philosophical speculations he had begun in his *Study of Thomas Hardy*. But these were more about the bases on which a healthy post-war society could be formed than about the war itself, and so abstruse that it is hardly surprising the magazine had no success. No more than a few individuals came to the proposed meetings, so that the whole enterprise quickly collapsed. By the time it did, however, Lawrence had been surprised by some news that gave him other, more immediate concerns to deal with than the future of post-war English society.

At the beginning of November 1915, a warrant was issued for the suppression of *The Rainbow*. How the authorities came to prosecute the novel was never quite clear. It may be that, aware of Lawrence's activities among anti-war groups, they were objecting to the scenes in which Ursula challenges the belief of her first lover, Anton Skrebensky, that it is his duty as a soldier to go to South Africa to fight against the Boers. The arguments she uses are similar to the ones Lawrence would employ to contest the need so many young men of his time felt to volunteer. Yet when Lady Ottoline's husband, Philip Morrell, who was an MP, asked in Parliament why the author of *The Rainbow* had been offered no opportunity to defend his novel before it was suppressed, the home secretary made it clear that the prosecution had not taken place under the very recent Defence of the Realm Act but under a statute against the publication of obscene material which dated back to the mid-nineteenth century. He also explained it was according to the provisions of this statute that it was the publishers of *The Rainbow* who were prosecuted rather than its author (it was one of Lawrence's bitter complaints that Methuen did nothing to defend the novel, but rather apologized for having published it in the first place).

In so far as the supposed obscenity of certain episodes or passages was in fact the issue, one could reasonably say that they were spoilt for choice. The chief concentration fell on a chapter called 'Shame' – an account of how Ursula has a lesbian relationship with one of her teachers at grammar school, which was signalled out in some early reviews for particular opprobrium – yet the details of how Will and Anna Brangwen spend most of their time in bed in the first days of their honeymoon are often daringly explicit. Later, when he is feeling emotionally abandoned by Anna, Will goes one evening into Nottingham and picks up a 'common girl' at the music hall. The way he then attempts to force himself on her is reminiscent of Paul Morel's efforts to force Clara to have sex with him in Chapter Twelve of *Sons and Lovers*. On Will's arrival back home, Anna recognizes his inflamed state and instinctively accepts that their marriage should enter a new stage, one in which the object is to exploit the other person's body for as much personal gratification as possible. In the passages that follow, Lawrence hints at practices his critics would call perverse and begins to employ a vocabulary for alluding to anal intercourse which he would continue to develop for the rest of his writing career. Compared with these, and some of the passages describing Ursula and Anton Skrebensky's lovemaking, there is nothing in 'Shame' that ought to have been found too alarming, even in 1915. If this chapter was in fact what triggered the prosecution, it must have been the very idea of lesbianism that shocked, rather than Lawrence's treatment of it.

More questionable in our day than Lawrence's dealings with lesbianism are the workings of what seems like a certain confusion, which could perhaps be traced back to his struggle with his own bisexual tendencies. In March 1915, he was invited by Russell to Cambridge and returned extremely distressed by the casual acceptance of homosexuality he felt he had detected there, especially in the behaviour of John Maynard Keynes, one of the principal figures in the so-called Bloomsbury group. The discovery gave him nightmares, he would confess, in which he was living in a world of beetles. A month or so later, the Lawrences had a visit from David ('Bunny') Garnett, who was accompanied by Augustine Birrell, a loquacious friend who made no secret of being in love with Garnett. Lawrence himself was very fond of 'Bunny', and, after the two friends had gone, wrote him a fervent letter in which he contested the claim one of them must have made that 'men loving men' did not really matter:

> It is so wrong, it is unbearable. It takes a form of inward corruption which truly makes me scarce able to live. Why is there this horrible sense of frowstiness, so repulsive, as if it came from deep inward dirt – a sort of sewer – deep in men like Keynes and Birrell and Duncan Grant . . . David, my dear . . . You can come away, and grow whole, and love a woman, and marry her, and make life good, and be happy . . . In the name of everything that is called love, leave this set and stop this blasphemy against love.[4]

One of the possible justifications for pronouncing authoritatively on someone else's emotional life is a profound understanding of the topics at issue which derives from personal experience. But Forster would claim that in writing the naked bathing scene in *The White Peacock* Lawrence had not known what he was doing, and there are indications that in 1915 he was not much clearer about the eroticism that seemed to enter into some of his own relationships with men. It is this lack of clarity which makes his treatment of same-sex relations in *The Rainbow* among that novel's few unsatisfactory aspects. One of Tom Brangwen's sons is also called Tom. When he attends the funeral of his father, who has been drowned in a flood that is felt to sweep away not only him but the old rural world he represents, he is seen through the eyes of his niece Ursula. Though he is a superficially attractive figure, there is nevertheless something about Uncle Tom she finds distasteful – signs of a gnawing inner dissatisfaction and a quality 'in all his elegant demeanour, bestial, almost corrupt'.[5] That homosexuality is the reason for this characterization is only hinted at, but the case is clearer with Winifred Inger, the school mistress with whom Ursula has an affair. During a crucial swimming-pool scene in 'Shame', she is described as beautiful: 'Ah, the beauty of the firm, white, cool flesh! Ah, the wonderful firm limbs,' thinks Ursula. 'If she could but hold them, hug them, press them between her own small breasts!' But once the affair is over, she schemes to bring together Winifred Inger with her Uncle Tom, in what she increasingly sees as their shared perversion.

Ursula and Winifred visit Tom at his ugly, recently built manager's house in the sprawling new pit town of Wiggiston. In *Sons and Lovers,* Lawrence had accepted the collieries as part and parcel of the Nottinghamshire landscape (Paul Morel even tells his mother at one point that he enjoys the sight of them). But now they are represented as a hideous blight on nature, inhabited by zombies, a kingdom of the dark cynically ruled over by Uncle Tom, who is still giving off his 'slight sense of putrescence'. Yet it is precisely because of this sense that he seems to Ursula an appropriate future partner for Winifred, of whose 'gross, ugly movements' she has now become aware. Instead of the attractive figure she had perceived in the swimming pool, there is now Winifred's 'clayey, inert, unquickened flesh, that reminded her of great prehistoric lizards'.[6] Of course, the alteration could merely be meant as an indication of how Ursula has changed her mind about her sexuality, but Lawrence's use of words like 'putrescence' and 'clayey', as well as his whole treatment of Uncle Tom, suggest a writer for whom same-sex relationships represent a challenge he finds it difficult to meet.

From almost the beginning of his return from Italy, Lawrence had begun to dream of establishing a colony in some faraway place where like-minded people could live their lives according to principles far different from those which obtained in England, especially an England at war. Rananim was the name he had for it and that he could describe with great confidence and enthusiasm how it would function is suggested by Aldous Huxley's later declaration that he was ready to enrol after only his first meeting with Lawrence. The United States was one of the possible locations for this colony, and that was where, with the prosecution of *The Rainbow* and the failure of *The Signature*, he had now made up his mind to go. He had a growing readership in the United States, and there might be publishers there who would be more inclined to take his future work than those in England wary of suffering the same fate as Methuen, which had paid Lawrence his advance but had then to stand by while copies of the novel which should have begun to ensure them a return were being seized and burnt.

At first the idea was to go to New York, where Pinker had publishing contacts, but then Lawrence's attention switched to Florida because the climate was believed more suitable and there seemed more possibility of eventually founding a colony. In either case, what he and Frieda needed were passports and, with the help of Lady Cynthia Asquith, he managed to secure these before a further difficulty arose. With conscription in the offing, it had become a condition of leaving the country that men of military age should 'attest' their willingness to serve in the armed forces, if required. Lawrence spent two hours in a queue waiting to do precisely this, but then decided it would be a hypocritical gesture and left. Meanwhile, in addition to Philip Morrell's questions in Parliament, several people were trying to put pressure on the authorities and have the decision on *The Rainbow* rescinded. By going to the United States, Lawrence felt he would be leaving them in the lurch. It was while everything was in this state of flux that John Davys Beresford, a novelist friend of Murry's who owned a cottage in Cornwall, said that the Lawrences could borrow it. Cornwall was not exactly the United States, but it must have seemed remote enough to represent an escape from what was happening in the country at large, and a convenient stopping-off point while the fate of *The Rainbow* was finally decided and any further difficulties about going to the United States were sorted out.

4
Cornwall and *Women in Love*

Lawrence was initially pleased to be in Cornwall. Beresford's comfortable holiday home was near Padstow and close to the sea. The vestiges Lawrence felt he perceived, in the people and landscape, of an ancient Celtic culture were comforting to someone who had decided that the continuing war was sounding the death knell of Western civilization – founded, as he believed it to have been, on the teachings of Plato and Jesus. Anything outside this orbit attracted him, whether it was the little that could be known about the druids, Indian and Middle Eastern philosophy, the Aztecs, the art of Japan and Africa or the pre-Socratic philosophers, like Anaximander and Heraclitus, he had recently been reading about. One effect of the war on him was to make him feel that he needed to find some intellectual and emotional standing ground quite separated from the catastrophic self-destruction he was witnessing (or at least hearing and reading about). When in March 1916 Beresford indicated that he would need his house back, Lawrence and Frieda moved further down the Cornish coast to a remote spot called Zennor. There, they were able to find a small cottage that could be rented unfurnished for only £5 a year. The cost was important because their resources were again running low, and in fact their situation in 1916 would have been desperate had not the rich American poet Amy Lowell, whom Lawrence had met in London, sent him a gift of £60, and Pinker another £50 as an advance on royalties unlikely to materialize in the near future.

Lawrence's satisfaction in his move away from London and the home counties was cut short by another bout of his now familiar

The Lawrences' cottage in Zennor.

winter sickness. Things were worse this time, in that allied to his usual chest problems was a feeling of numbness down one side of his body that seriously alarmed both him and Frieda (were he to die, she would have quite literally nowhere to go and would risk being interned as an enemy alien). One of the new friends they had made on their return to England was a poet called Dollie Radford, one of whose children was a doctor. It was probably in response to an appeal from Frieda that Maitland Radford made the long journey to Zennor in order to examine Lawrence. He found the patient weak and run down but with nothing 'organically' wrong with him – a diagnosis which implies that he had ruled out TB. He was not, of course, in a position to undertake the kind of rigorous examination that would have involved sputum tests and X-rays but, because TB was endemic, he must already have been familiar with its symptoms. In any case, if he had detected the disease, he would have been under a legal obligation as a doctor to report it.

The Zennor cottage was in a block of three and next door to a larger building, from the top of which one had a clearer view of the sea. None of the other buildings were occupied, so there was the potential here for a small colony of the kind Lawrence had dreamt of establishing in the United States. The only person to join him and Frieda for any length of time during their first months in Cornwall, however, was a young man who had recently graduated from Oxford, called Philip Heseltine. As fiercely opposed to the war as Lawrence, and captivated by the latter's brilliance both on paper and in person, Heseltine would later become well known in the music world under the name of Peter Warlock – but at the beginning of 1916, he was still looking to find his way and was in a distraught emotional state. Either at Garsington or in London, he had met a young Swiss woman employed by Lady Ottoline to look after her daughter, and had fallen in love with her. The trouble was that he was already in a relationship with an artist's model called Minnie Channing, who was pregnant by him. No less reluctant to give young people advice than he had been in the case of Bunny Garnett (although he was only 32 himself), Lawrence diagnosed in Heseltine a familiar split between a yearning for spiritual values, which his infatuation with the Swiss woman represented, and the more earthy appeal of 'Puma', as Channing was known. After Puma had come to stay with the Lawrences for a while, Lawrence reported that he was inclined to advise the young man to stick by her.

   Heseltine stayed seven weeks with the Lawrences in Cornwall, and was joined there for shorter stays by not only Channing, but another of his friends, an Armenian called Dikran Kouyoumdjian. Having worked with Lawrence on a scheme to have *The Rainbow* published privately, which would come to nothing, Heseltine seems to have left Zennor feeling some resentment at the interference in his private affairs. 'Lawrence is a very great artist,' he wrote to another of the older men he admired, Frederick Delius, 'but hard and autocratic in his views and outlook.'[1] He had taken with him from Zennor the manuscript of the successor to *Study of Thomas Hardy*, the latest version of Lawrence's philosophy. This was called *Goats and Compasses*, which is a sign very occasionally seen outside pubs, but in this case seems to have been a way of suggesting an antinomy between animality and high intellectual endeavour.

Heseltine's later report that there was a great deal in this text about homosexuality seems likely enough, since that is a topic which preoccupied Lawrence throughout this period, but so resentful had Heseltine become that he may well have destroyed the manuscript. Whatever other copies there were also disappeared, so quite what stage Lawrence's philosophy had reached in *Goats and Compasses* will never be known precisely.

How to make a living after the disaster of *The Rainbow* must have preoccupied Lawrence greatly. In the summer, he would publish a collection of what was mostly his earlier poetry and call it *Amores*; it was then also that *Twilight in Italy* appeared. The difference of this from a conventional travel book can be illustrated by the chapter called 'The Theatre', which had initially appeared in the *English Review* as an amusing essay about a group of travelling actors who had visited Gargnano while he and Frieda were living there and performed several plays, including *Hamlet*. When Lawrence came to revise it for *Twilight in Italy*, its length was doubled. This was because the actors' visit was now enveloped in his philosophy, and Hamlet's 'to be, or not to be' was taken to represent a choice between the old pagan belief in the primacy of the self – with its accompanying reliance on the flesh and its association with autocracy – and, on the other hand, a situation where, because of Christianity, 'I am dead unto myself, but I live in the Infinite' (this last being a feeling Lawrence associates, for reasons it would take pages to elucidate, with democracy and industrialization). According to him, the opposition of these two positions is not only the most significant philosophic event of the Renaissance but one which *Hamlet* enacts:

> At the Renaissance (the) great Half-Truth overcame the other great Half-Truth. The Christian Infinite, reached by a process of abnegation, a process of being absorbed, dissolved, diffused into the great Not-Self, supplanted the old pagan Infinite . . . There is only one Infinite, the world now cried, there is the great Christian Infinite of renunciation and consummation in the not-self. The other, that old pride, is damnation.[2]

How *Hamlet* comes to exemplify all this is difficult to understand, but for Lawrence, 'the whole play is the tragedy of the convulsed reaction of the mind from the flesh, of the spirit from the self, the reaction from the great aristocratic to the great democratic principle.'[3] Most of the original travel sketches are amplified in ways similar to those apparent in 'The Theatre'. Although – together with additional, previously unpublished work – these made *Twilight in Italy* a more substantial book, they were hardly likely to bring him nearer to being the bestselling author he desperately felt he now needed to be.

What was required above all was another novel, and, ignoring the dispiriting nature of his publishing prospects, Lawrence had begun in April to revise and rewrite whatever material he still had left over from *The Sisters*, always referring to it as his 'sequel' to *The Rainbow*. What is surprising is just how different from its predecessor *Women in Love* turned out to be. At its opening, Ursula Brangwen has become a teacher at her local grammar school, while her sister Gudrun is temporarily back in her native regions after having enjoyed some success as an artist in London. In one of the many conversations that make this work so much more of an ongoing debate than its predecessor, these two emancipated young women, with careers that make them self-sufficient, are discussing the pros and cons of marriage in a way that would have been impossible for young women fifty years earlier. The two men with whom they become involved – Rupert Birkin, a school inspector of a kind Lawrence himself might conceivably have become had he stayed in the teaching profession, and Gerald Crich, the son of a local mine owner – are also often heard debating marriage as well as other more abstruse topics.

Whatever old material Lawrence was working with, it was not long before he made use of much more recent experiences and incorporated someone who is very like Heseltine into his novel. In a chapter entitled 'Crême de Menthe', Gerald takes his friend Rupert to a café in London where artists congregate. There he meets a man called Halliday, who invites them both back to his flat. The Indian servant who greets them is someone Lawrence would have met when he had visited Heseltine before coming to Cornwall, just as the artefacts he describes as being in the flat are ones he would have seen then. That Halliday is indeed a (far-from-flattering) portrait of Heseltine should be obvious from the latter's angry response to his depiction when *Women in Love* finally appeared, and from the way the character is shown in the novel as entangled in a difficult relationship with an artist's model, clearly based on Channing. In describing that relationship, Lawrence includes a detail that he must have had from either one or other of them: that Heseltine had given Channing £100 to find some way of dealing with her pregnancy, a detail that they cannot have been happy to see made public.

'Crême de Menthe' offers a vivid and highly effective sketch of London's Bohemia, just as elsewhere there are shrewd insights into the English aristocracy in its more liberal, intellectual manifestations and a probing picture of the coal-mining industry. There is a degree of social range here which makes *Women in Love* far more of a 'state of the nation' novel than *The Rainbow* had been, and various aspects of English society are presented in what is largely a succession of arresting tableaux (the 'pictorial' aspect of the novel is evident in the detailed descriptions of several paintings and sculptures as well as of the brightly coloured clothes the female characters wear). The setting remains pre-war – but, conscious that the tone of the novel as well as some of its episodes are often charged with extremes of emotional violence, and that Rupert Birkin periodically expresses a profound misanthropy as well as referring on one occasion to the satisfaction it would give him to see mankind exterminated, Lawrence later wrote a foreword to the novel in which he explained that it 'took its final shape in the midst of a period of war' and that he therefore hoped 'the bitterness of the war may be taken for granted in the characters'.[4]

Unscrupulous in using people he knew as models for characters in his fiction, the way Lawrence did so depended a great deal on how major or minor those characters happened to be. Halliday is clearly a minor figure, but that is not the case with Hermione Roddice, a local aristocrat who is given many of the physical attributes, mannerisms and tastes in dress of Lady Ottoline Morrell. Like

Lady Ottoline, Hermione brings together in her country house a group of artists and intellectuals, one of whom is an unmistakeable brief portrait of Bertrand Russell. Yet the more fictional characters become involved in a narrative, the more the features of the model have to change to suit the circumstances. Roddice has been the mistress of Birkin, and she is represented as becoming increasingly upset by the indifference with which he is beginning to treat her. When they are alone together during one of her house parties and Birkin is ignoring her by becoming absorbed in a book, she comes from behind and hits him once over the head with a lapis lazuli paperweight, and would have hit him again had he not been able, even in his dazed state, to avoid a second blow and the serious injury and perhaps death that would follow.

Lady Ottoline was outraged when she read a manuscript copy of *Women in Love*. Since Hermione had been given so many of her own outward characteristics, it must have crossed her mind that that there were some readers who might think she had indeed been Lawrence's mistress, and she complained openly about the point in the novel where she is made to seem homicidal. But just as there are elements in the character of Hermione which would seem to derive from Jessie Chambers (her soulfulness, for example), so the violence she exhibits is much more likely to derive from Frieda than from Lady Ottoline. There is in fact a record that after Lawrence had thought one of the violent quarrels they tended to have in Cornwall was over, Frieda came up behind him when he was washing up and broke a heavy plate over his head.[5]

In the novel, after escaping from Hermione's house and rolling naked in the grass, Birkin decides that she was justified in venting her frustration in a life-threatening manner, and this is a view in tune with those he has expressed elsewhere. He is an advocate of the idea that the only true morality lies in people acting spontaneously from their deepest, most genuine impulses, whatever those impulses might be and whatever the cost to others. As Lawrence himself was to put in a letter in 1917, in a slightly different context, 'Desire is holy, belonging to the mystic unknown, no matter *what* the desire.'[6] He was conscious that in expressing notions of this kind he would be regarded by many as a crank, and there is certainly a view that the suppression of *The Rainbow*, anxieties generated by the war, relative isolation, difficulties in his relationship with Frieda, illness and poverty all conspired to make a highly sensitive individual mentally unstable during this period. One possible argument against this is the way that, in *Women in Love*, Lawrence provides a context for Birkin in which his unusual ideas are contested by those around him (the idea being that no one able to do this could have entirely lost that sense of where one stands in the world which the mentally unstable tend to lack). Gerald is one character who disagrees with Birkin, but his chief intellectual antagonist is Ursula, especially when it comes to the topic of marriage, already announced as a major theme of the novel in her opening conversation with Gudrun.

Lawrence had believed that during coition between heterosexuals male and female were merged together, and that, in one of his confusedly varied scenarios, a sign of their success would be the way that, afterwards, each party would have developed a more refined and developed individuality. It was a formula difficult to apply to the repeated sex likely to occur in any marriage or long-term relationship. Struggling unsuccessfully to leave the concept of 'love' out altogether, Birkin frequently expresses his fear of being enveloped by a woman, of the female as Magna Mater, and proposes to Ursula a marriage in which, on the one hand, the male should be the dominant partner while, on the other, both of them should be like two stars in the sky, separate but balanced, distinct and together, as it were. Not unreasonably, she can neither make anything of this nor warm to Birkin's idea that, in addition to marriage with her, he needs a close and intimate relationship with another man, the kind of *blutsbrüdershaft* that he proposes to Gerald, but that Gerald rejects. In a prologue Lawrence wrote for *Women in Love* but never published, Birkin is described as someone who goes through phases in which 'it was for men that he felt the hot, flushing roused attraction which a man is supposed to feel for the other sex.'[7] The scene in which he and Gerald wrestle naked forms part of Birkin's effort to persuade his friend to become a third party to the marriage with Ursula he hopes soon to enjoy, a position Gerald is no more keen to accept than she is to believe necessary. Her union with Birkin is nonetheless represented as eventually successful, the one bright spot in an otherwise gloomy picture, but Lawrence is far less effective at convincing the reader how that could be so than in showing why the quite deliberately contrasted relationship of Gerald and Gudrun is destined to fail.

In an early episode that says a lot about Lawrence's method for establishing character in *Women in Love*, Ursula is watching butterflies while her sister sketches the dark, turgid plants growing in the mud at the side of a lake. These *fleurs du mal* fascinate Gudrun, and she is shown as aware of the decadence of the artistic world to which she essentially belongs but happy enough to make the most of the sensations she encounters as she travels along what Birkin refers to as a 'river of dissolution'. Her relationship with Gerald is largely a sadomasochistic one, and another detailed and convincing exploration by Lawrence along one of the less frequented byways of sexuality. The situation she is in might suggest that she is inevitably the weaker partner, like the artist's model in that early scene in Halliday's flat who, after Gerald has slept with her, has the look of a 'violated slave, whose fulfilment lies in her further and further violation' and who makes 'his nerves quiver with acutely desirable sensation.'[8] But the 'Pussum' is in fact far stronger than Gerald, as Gudrun also proves to be. This is partly because both women understand their own natures far better than he understands his own, and because he has an emotional dependence powerfully dramatized by Lawrence in scenes of his lovemaking with Gudrun in the ski chalet near the end of the novel. As one of Lawrence's most successful creations, Gudrun lies at the far end of that continuum which represents his reliance on his friends and acquaintances for his fictional characters. Halliday is a reasonably direct portrait of Heseltine; Hermione Roddice bears a strong resemblance to Lady Ottoline but is called on to play a part in *Women in Love* involving attitudes and actions that she would never have dreamt of. For Gudrun, Lawrence borrowed a few characteristics of Katherine Mansfield, but the overall result is so different that it is not surprising she did not recognize herself when the novel finally appeared.

After Heseltine left Zennor, Lawrence redoubled efforts to persuade Murry and Mansfield to come and live close by. They were then in a relatively stable phase of their on-off relationship and living in Bandol, in the south of France. Mansfield was reluctant to leave there but allowed herself to be convinced that being close to the Lawrences would be stimulating, and she and Murry arrived in Zennor in April 1916. They stayed a little over two months before admitting to themselves that the experiment had not been a success and moving across the Cornish peninsula to its south side. One thing that Mansfield in particular could not bear was having to be privy to the Lawrences' violent quarrels. She describes in a letter how on one occasion Frieda came running into their house screaming for Murry to save her and pursued by a Lawrence white with fury and beating his wife about the body whenever he could catch up with her. What especially baffled Mansfield was how easily, when the two parties had calmed down, they reverted to being affectionate towards each other, as if nothing had happened. Lawrence was fond of Mansfield and respected her as the sort of genuinely creative person he thought Murry wasn't. In *Women in Love*, Gudrun is also represented as a genuine artist, but one whose undoubted talent always expresses itself in small-scale sculptures, just as Mansfield's did in her short stories.

Murry was dark-haired and slightly shorter than Lawrence, so not at all in physique like the blond, athletic character Gerald Crich, who has attached to him, in the fashion of a Wagnerian opera, a motif of those icy heights where he is eventually to lose his life. But in his reminiscences of being with Lawrence in Cornwall, Murry does indicate that he had been offered that position of third party in a marriage which Birkin is thinking of for Gerald.[9] There seems no doubt that Lawrence was physically attracted to Murry but also that, after he had left Zennor, his interest in a young man from a neighbouring farming family, seven years younger than himself, strengthened. William Hocking had an enquiring mind but very little formal education, and Lawrence spent long periods helping

William Henry Hocking.

him to bring in the harvest in 1916, and more particularly in the following year. The experience must have reminded him of the happy times he had spent with Alan Chambers, to whom he often seems to have been more physically drawn than to Alan's sister Jessie. Working in the fields with another man whose intellectual development he could assist appears to have made Lawrence unusually happy, but that these relationships ever became fully physical seems highly unlikely given the men involved. Like Murry, Chambers and Hocking were uncomplicated heterosexuals, while Lawrence's writing shows that he was often struggling at this time with his own sexual nature. In a further extension of his philosophy, which he began writing after *Goats and Compasses,* Lawrence would echo Birkin and write, 'I shall accept all my desires and repudiate none' but also 'I must make my peace with the serpent of abhorrence that is within me. I must own my most secret shame and my most secret shameful desire.'[10] It is not clear whether the reference here is to same-sex desire, but the context, both biographical and literary, makes it likely.

The departure of Murry and Mansfield left the Lawrences isolated again, but from time to time they were visited by a few faithful friends from London who included Catherine Carswell, Dollie Radford and Barbara Low, Ivy Low's aunt, with whom Lawrence could talk about psychoanalysis. Around Christmas and into 1917, they were also able to welcome two American admirers, a journalist called Robert Mountsier and his girlfriend Esther Andrews, who was also a writer (Andrews would stay on after Mountsier left and, like Ivy Low before her, cause Frieda some anxiety because of her obvious admiration for Lawrence's gifts). The presence of these two Americans reignited Lawrence's interest in escaping to their country and helped him to conceive a new project, in which he decided to analyse and celebrate the great American writers in a book that would later appear under the title *Studies in Classic American Literature*. With Mountsier's help, he made plans to sail to the United States in March 1917, spend a short time in New York to establish publishing contacts there and then press on to some remote spot on the Pacific Coast. He could not do all that, however, without first having both his and Frieda's passports renewed.

With the war showing no signs of coming to an end, and Lady Cynthia Asquith's father-in-law replaced as prime minister by the more energetic and bellicose David Lloyd George at the end of 1916, the government's control over its citizens was becoming stricter. The introduction of conscription obliged Lawrence to undergo what was a second medical inspection in 1916, and he would be called to a third in the following year. It was perhaps not too surprising that, in this state of affairs, Lawrence was not able to have the passports renewed, and by the middle of 1917 he was having to reconcile himself to staying in Cornwall. A partially mollified Heseltine – who had been declared unfit for conscription and had not yet, perhaps, read the portrait of himself in *Women in Love* – had returned to the area along with a friend, also very interested in music, called Cecil Gray. Gray had rented a large house on the sea, around 6.5 kilometres (4 mi.) from the Lawrences' cottage, and would provide new company for them.

Also in their part of Cornwall at this time was a writer who went by the name of Meredith Starr. He and his wife, Mary, were among the many in this period heavily involved in the movement known as Occultism. This has very many different aspects, but a key text for its members was a book by the Russian mystic Madame Blavatsky entitled *The Secret Doctrine*. This claimed to reconcile items of Hindu philosophy with modern Western science, talked of a special esoteric knowledge once known only to a small number of initiates all over the world, and offered a spiritual escape route for those who could no longer accept orthodox Christian doctrine but did not want to surrender to materialism. The Occultists were very interested in magical rituals from the past, and although Lawrence claimed that Meredith and Mary Starr were too eccentric for his taste, he was clearly drawn to what they had to say, especially on the subject of health and the way transcendence could be achieved within the individual human body. The book that impressed him was not so much Blavatsky's but an interpretation of the Book of Revelation called *The Apocalypse Unsealed* by one of her associates, James Pryse. It was from Pryse that Lawrence took the idea of

Madame Blavatsky (1831–1891).

kundalini, now the name for a kind of yoga, but for Pryse a way of marshalling cosmic energy from the various nerve centres, or *chakras*, in the body. Lawrence would later rely on the notion of *chakras* to posit what he calls 'the biological psyche' in his books on psychoanalysis, but the ideas he found in Pryse and other Occultists began to surface in his third attempt to write his philosophy, which he was making in 1917. The book in which they featured was called *At the Gates*, and since, like *Goats and Compasses*, it has disappeared, it is now only known to us from a series of essays he had published in the *English Review* under the title 'The Reality of Peace'.

The last of the 'Reality of Peace' essays finds Lawrence struggling with his old dilemma of how to reconcile merging with separation, lapsing out with individuality and even love with hate. After a few phrases about how a male child is 'born uncreated' but slowly extricates himself into the 'singleness of manhood', he goes on:

And I set out to meet the other, the unknown of womanhood.
I give myself to the love that makes me join and fuse towards a
universal oneness, I give myself to the hate that makes me detach
myself, extricate myself vividly from the other in sharp passion;
I am given up into fellowship and communion. I am distinguished
in keen resistance and isolation, both so utterly, so exquisitely,
that I am and I am not at once; suddenly I lapse out of the duality
into a sheer beauty of fulfilment, I am a rose of lovely peace.[11]

Hate is a surprising and relatively new element here, but otherwise this is the old insistence on how sexual intercourse can bring fulfilment, although there could not have been many readers of the *English Review* who could understand what Lawrence was talking about. The rose is a key symbol in Occultism, even if Lawrence's growing interest in the movement is not very evident in this particular extract. It becomes more obvious in the chapter in *Women in Love* ('Excurse') in which Ursula and Birkin finally commit to each other and where both are described as reaching that 'sheer beauty of fulfilment' mentioned here.

After a violent quarrel, Ursula and Birkin are found in 'Excurse' taking tea before an open fire in a coaching inn. She kneels to embrace him round the loins and rest her head on his thigh:

It was a perfect passing away for both of them, and at the same time the most intolerable accession into being, the marvellous fullness of immediate gratification, overwhelming, outflooding from the source of the deepest life-force, the darkest, deepest life-source of the human body, at the back and base of the loins.

The reference here would seem to be to the *chakra* or nerve centre in the lower back, at the base of the spine, and Lawrence has Ursula meditate further on its significance a little further on:

There were strange fountains of his body, more mysterious and potent than any she had imagined or known, more satisfying, ah, finally, mystically-physically satisfying. She had thought there was no source deeper than the phallic source. And, now, behold, from the strange marvellous flanks and thighs, further in mystery than the phallic source, came the floods of ineffable darkness and ineffable riches.

One might have thought that, to achieve this powerful effect, something rather more than an embrace must have gone on, but that seems impossible given where Birkin and Ursula are. That they do soon have sex, however, is made clear a little later when, having decided to resign their jobs so that they can go away together, they leave the inn and head into the countryside (for even a minimum of clarity, many admirers of Lawrence have to quote more of his writing in this vein than they would like to, and yet not enough to demonstrate quite how unintelligible he could sometimes be):

> They threw off all their clothes, and he gathered her to him, and found her, found the pure lambent reality of her forever invisible flesh . . . She had her desire of him, she touched, she received the maximum of unspeakable communication in touch, dark, subtle, positively silent, a magnificent gift . . . She had her desire fulfilled, he had his desire fulfilled. For she was to him what he was to her, the immemorial magnificence of mystic, palpable, real otherness.[12]

Here, the singleness which is contingent on, or perhaps even continuous with, satisfying intercourse seems something that can be appreciated by a partner as well as oneself.

Ursula and Birkin represent the positive pole of love and marriage in *Women in Love*, yet, as I have already suggested, Lawrence is far more convincing when working at the opposite extreme: in describing Gerald's brief affair with the artist's model, but also (for example) in the way, after the death of his father, he goes to Gudrun's house at night and more or less obliges her to have 'comfort sex' with him. In *The Rainbow*, he had written two extraordinary passages that describe how Anton Skrebensky emerges shattered from having sex with the harpy Ursula has briefly become, and Gudrun eventually has a similar effect on Gerald. Because Birkin is so patently an alter ego of Lawrence, it is easy to forget how he is also drawing on his own complicated nature (and the complicated nature of his relationship with Frieda) in describing Gerald and the way in which, in their final encounters in the ski chalet, his dependence on Gudrun leads to his suicide. These are powerfully written episodes, and, by contrast with them, those involving Ursula and Birkin's lovemaking are often full of windy rhetoric and unconvincing assertions: they make claims for how togetherness can be reconciled with singleness that are not borne out by anything that is represented with any clarity. This means that the uplift their relationship is designed to provide at the conclusion of what is a profoundly pessimistic novel does not materialize. Lawrence had already ended *The Rainbow* on a defiantly optimistic note, hardly justified by the situation Ursula finally finds herself in; at the conclusion of *Women in Love* there are similar suggestions of a brighter future, for Ursula and Birkin at least. Yet, given what we have been shown of the tensions in their relationship, it is hard to be optimistic. Indeed, insofar as these two characters *are* based on Lawrence and Frieda, it seems that he could only somewhat desperately hope that there were better times coming.

The Lawrences' new friend in Cornwall Cecil Gray was more than an important social resource, since it is possible that, while Lawrence was preoccupied with William Hocking at the farm, Frieda may have slept with him. When the Lawrences went together to visit Gray at his large house by the sea, they would spend some of their time singing German songs. On one of these occasions, they were interrupted by local officials complaining that a light was shining intermittently from one of the house's sea-facing windows, in contravention of the blackout regulations then being enforced (it was a time when there were a renewed number of effective attacks by German submarines off the Cornish coast). The worry of the officials was that these strange newcomers to the area, one of whom was in fact German and all of whom made no effort to keep quiet their opposition to the war, might be signalling to the enemy; they feared that they might be part of that 'fifth column' the more jingoistic elements in the British press often worried about. Following this episode with Gray, who was fined £20, the police arrived at the Lawrences' cottage to search it, and shortly afterwards the couple was ordered to leave Cornwall more or less immediately (by 15 October 1917). Their Cornish days were abruptly over, and although Lawrence later made efforts to get back to Cornwall, he never did.

5
Orphans of the Storm

The Lawrences' expulsion from Cornwall meant leaving behind accommodation they had already paid for, as well as many of their few belongings. Arriving in London as orphans of the storm, they were housed for a short while by Dollie Radford in Hampstead but were then very quickly offered a room in a house in Mecklenburgh Square by the American poet Hilda Doolittle. Lawrence had known 'H. D.' before going to Cornwall and got on well with her. She was in an open marriage with another poet, Richard Aldington, who was serving in the army and came home occasionally on leave, when he would sleep not with his wife but with his American mistress, Arabella Yorke, who was also staying in the house.

After the relative isolation of Cornwall, this was a heady mix, diversified by visits to the opera which Lady Cynthia Asquith was able to arrange for the Lawrences. Contributing to it was the strong feeling H. D. began to develop for Lawrence and the arrival of Cecil Gray, who appears to have set his sights on Frieda (although H. D. would later go to live with Gray in Cornwall and become pregnant by him). Around this time, Lawrence began a new novel which would become *Aaron's Rod*. In it, a colliery worker called Aaron Sisson decides at Christmas to abandon his wife and children and sets out to fend for himself, with only his flute playing to rely on for his livelihood. Very early on, he is shown as falling in with a varied group of middle-class Bohemians, just like those in Mecklenburgh Square. In one scene, a character who is quite clearly modelled on H. D. is at the opera openly discussing with her husband and others whether she should go to live in Dorset with someone equally

Richard Aldington (1892–1962), English writer and poet.

obviously based on Gray, the change of county being the only concession to confidentiality Lawrence makes. But *Aaron's Rod* was then to hang fire for a long time after Lawrence began writing it, waiting, as it were, for further developments in its author's personal life which he could use to carry it on.

In December 1917, the Lawrences left the imbroglios of London and went to live in a remote village in Berkshire appropriately called Hermitage (it was near Newbury). Dollie Radford owned a cottage there, which she and her family only occasionally used; initially, at least, she seems to have let Lawrence and Frieda have it rent free. From then until the winter of 1919, they were chiefly to alternate between this house and an even more remote one on the edge of the Peak District in Derbyshire called Mountain Cottage that had been secured for them by Lawrence's loyal sister Ada, who lived in nearby Ripley and paid the rent. Her help was invaluable at a time of continual money troubles for her brother. He received a random trickle of small amounts when certain of his poems, essays or short stories were published, but never enough to prevent a humiliating dependence on what was essentially charity. It was after Christmas that he made a second application to the Royal Literary Fund, the result of which was, in July 1918, another handout of £50. He had hoped for more, and his response – 'a miserable £50 from that dirty Royal Literary Fund' – is perhaps best taken as an indication of how uncomfortable he found it to be so reliant on others for keeping body and soul together.[1]

A sign that Lawrence was far from unwilling to try to help himself was the contract he managed to secure to write a history textbook for schools. He laboured away at *Movements in European History*, as the result was called, often with great reluctance, and had finished it in April 1919, when he must have felt that the £50 it would bring on submission had been well earned. More congenial was the work he had continued to do on his essays on American writers. He had started these in Cornwall and carried on with them after his expulsion. One of the ideas dominating them was that all literature necessarily partakes of the spirit of the place in which it is conceived. This meant that when Europeans first arrived in America they brought with them ideals in conflict with that continent's 'spirit of place', and that they therefore had tended to produce work reflective of this division. 'What Hawthorne deliberately says in *The Scarlet Letter*' Lawrence writes in an introduction to his essays, 'is on the whole a falsification of what he unconsciously says in his art language.'¹ This claim illustrates not only his idea about why the great American writers should have turned out to be so different from their European contemporaries (despite many apparent similarities), but a literary critical principle he employs throughout his essays and sums up neatly in their final version with 'Never trust the artist, trust the tale.'²

Between November 1918 and June 1919, the *English Review* published eight of the essays, which, much revised, would appear in Lawrence's *Studies in Classic American Literature* in 1923. These included specific studies of Benjamin Franklin, Hector St. John de Crevecoeur, James Fenimore Cooper and Edgar Allan Poe, as well as Nathaniel Hawthorne. Missing at this stage were essays on Richard Henry Dana and Herman Melville, and various attempts Lawrence would make to round the work off with an essay on Walt Whitman. There were two main reasons why Whitman had been, and remained in this period, a vitally significant figure for Lawrence. The first related to the American's homosexual feelings, his 'love of comrades' and the way his expression of them was a stimulus to Lawrence's attempts to come to terms with the erotic elements in his own relationships with men; but the second comes from the fact that it was chiefly in reading Whitman that Lawrence felt he could release himself from the shackles of rhyme and regular verse structure in poetry. He had begun his career as a poet by expressing what was recognizably 'modern' material in forms conventional enough to make Eddie Marsh more than happy to include him in his anthologies of 'Georgian' poetry. Through Ezra Pound and then more especially through Amy Lowell, Lawrence had been taken up by the imagists, although only a few of his poems could reasonably be said to correspond to the principles of their short-lived movement. As he was ready to admit, remembering and re-reading Walt Whitman led Lawrence to the realization that it was free verse along Whitman's lines which would provide the best medium for his concerns. The collection he published in 1917, called *Look! We Have Come Through!* in reference to his struggles to establish an enduring relationship with his wife, is Whitmanesque in the relatively loose nature of its free verse but also, perhaps, its willingness to lay bare

Walt Whitman, 1887, photographed by George C. Cox in New York.

intimate details of his private life. Bertrand Russell's response when he heard about this collection – that he was glad Lawrence had come through but didn't see why he should look – is often regarded by Lawrentians as cheap, but if Lawrence was willing to sacrifice the privacies of others for the sake of his writing, he was equally ready to expose his own in ways which were startling but not always or inevitably of general interest.

He was still trying to get back to Cornwall – or, should that not be possible, to at least sublet the cottage (there was a point when Virginia Woolf and her husband showed some interest). Meanwhile, Hermitage was comfortable enough, even when Lawrence was laid low by one of his recurrent chest complaints, or when the cottage he and Frieda occupied had to be temporarily vacated because one or other of the Radfords was coming down. On those occasions, the Lawrences would find lodgings in the village, an apparent drawback that at least helped them get to know their neighbours better. Bordering a wood on the edge of the village was a small farm run by two women, and one of the many difficulties they had was in trying to protect their hens from being killed by foxes. The Lawrences became friendly with these two, and they provided Lawrence with material for a short story, later expanded into a novella, which he called *The Fox*. In its original, shorter version, a young man comes back from the war to a farm where he once lived with his grandfather and finds two women, about ten years older than himself, in charge. He realizes that by marrying one of them he can, as it were, repossess the property, while the woman he has chosen to approach, associating in her mind the young man with the fox she had once glimpsed but found too fascinating to shoot, sleepwalks into accepting his proposal (how much he actually cares for her is not made clear).

One of the more obvious meanings of this story is the reassertion of male prerogative in a world that, because of the war, had become temporarily dominated by women. In one of their early encounters in *Women in Love*, Birkin and Ursula watch a tomcat bullying a female into submission. Ursula reacts strongly to the idea that this ought to be a model for their own relationship, and indeed, later in the novel, Birkin seems to accept that they need to be in a partnership of give and take, of mutual love. Yet he never quite abandons his belief that men should lead, just as he never quite gives up on the idea of a close relation with another man, additional to marriage. This first idea remained Lawrence's own also for quite some time, as is suggested by his writing, in his essay on Hawthorne, that 'when woman is the leader or dominant in the sex relationship . . . then the activity of man is an activity of destruction and undoing' and, later, that a woman 'can never give expression to the profound movements of her own being. These movements can only find an expression through a man.'[3] Inclined as Lawrence was to what would now be called male chauvinism, it was perhaps fortunate that he had a wife always ready to scoff at notions of male supremacy. Towards the end of his life, he met an old friend in Eastwood who had the temerity to ask him why he had not married Jessie Chambers. 'I should have had too easy a life,' he replied, 'everything my own way, and my genius would have been destroyed.'[4]

When the young soldier returns to the farm in *The Fox*, he first suggests that he can find a lodging in the village pub but is told this will not be possible because all its inmates have been struck down by the flu. The reference is to the influenza epidemic that swept through the world's war-weakened populations in both 1918 and 1919, killing an estimated 50 million people. Lawrence was fortunate to avoid it on its first winter appearance in England, but very nearly died of it on its second. He and Frieda had begun their occupancy of Mountain Cottage in May 1918. When he fell dangerously ill early in the following year it was Ada who nursed him, in her house in Ripley. This was no doubt because it was better to be in town and closer to doctors when dealing with a life-threatening sickness, but it was also the case – in Lawrence's view, certainly, but also in that of those around him – that Frieda was not much of a carer. When he was feeling a little better and moved from Ripley back to Mountain Cottage, Ada went with him, because, in Lawrence's own words, she 'was the responsible nurse' and he was not going to be 'left to Frieda's tender mercies' until he was well again.[5] During their time in Derbyshire, Frieda periodically went back south on her own, on some occasions to attend the few meetings with her children which the law allowed, but on others chiefly to get away from her irascible husband.

When the armistice was declared in November 1918, both the Lawrences were in London and could attend an armistice party and meet old friends. Frieda was naturally anxious to get to Germany as soon as possible in order to see her family, but it would not prove possible to obtain the necessary documents for travelling before a peace treaty had been signed, which happened in June of the following year. Meanwhile, Lawrence was thinking yet again of the United States, where there seemed to be far more opportunities for his writing than in Britain, and thought he might travel directly there and wait for Frieda to join him later. *The Rainbow* had been published in the United States, and he was almost continuously in negotiations to find an American home for *Women in Love*, while it was, of course, also for the States that he had always intended his *Studies in Classic American Literature*. In the meantime, when he was not in Hermitage, he was back on his own turf. Mountain Cottage was only a few miles from Ripley, which was not very far from Eastwood. There, Willie Hopkin, the old friend who would ask why he had not married Jessie, was a committed and active socialist organizer and able to give him detailed information about the industrial unrest rife in the Midlands coalfields at this time. The Russian Revolution had increased Lawrence's apprehension that there would soon be a defining clash between Capital and Labour, and he had quickly dashed off a play on this topic entitled *Touch and Go*.

Instead of creating new characters for this play, Lawrence borrowed almost all of them from *Women in Love*: Gerald Crich has his second name changed to Barlow, Birkin is called Oliver Turton and Gudrun becomes Anabel Wrath. The result is hardly a success and has a particularly weak and inclusive finale, in which Turton tells a group of angry miners, who are complaining that Barlow and his like have all the wealth and power, 'As for power, somebody must have it, you know. It only rests with you to put it into the hands of the best men, the men you *really* believe in – and as for money, it's life, it's living that matters, not simply having money.'[6] Simple-minded though these remarks might seem as a response to industrial turmoil, they are not far from Lawrence's own view on the clash between Capital and Labour. He found it difficult to take sides, because he wanted to see the whole industrial system swept away and had utopian dreams of ideal communities, the economic bases of which were always left a little hazy.

Because he was a miner's son and wrote so well about the mining community, it was often assumed he must have been on the Left in politics. But that was far from being always the case. Douglas Goldring was an early admirer who had once worked for the *English Review*. A keen socialist, he helped launch a series of publications called *The People's Theatre*, in which he enthusiastically included *Touch and Go*, but this was no more a natural home for the play than Amy Lowell's imagist anthologies were for Lawrence's shorter poems. If he leaned in any one perceivable political direction during the war, it was to the Right rather than Left. 'Like you,' he wrote to his German sister-in-law in 1919, 'I don't believe in a vulgar democracy, lording it over life . . . I believe in the elect.'[7] So, apparently, does the Birkin figure in *Touch and Go*, but whom what he calls 'the best men' are, and how they might be chosen, were problems Lawrence would continue to puzzle over for the next few years.

If *Touch and Go* was poor, other consequences of Lawrence's return to his roots were much more fruitful. Two short stories that belong to this period are 'Fanny and Annie' and 'Tickets Please!'. In the first, a young woman who has thought to better herself by taking a job in a wealthy cultured household in the south makes a disappointed return to the Midlands and to a boyfriend she has left dangling there. Harry Goodall is good looking, and Fanny certainly finds him physically attractive, but he is also what she thinks of as 'common' and quite without ambition to be anything other. The climax of the story comes when Fanny goes to attend the service at the local chapel where she and Harry first met ten years ago, and where he still sings in the choir. There is a light brushing of humour as he is described as singing away 'like a canary', but then a sensation as a woman in the church suddenly stands up to denounce him. How dare he stand there, 'singing solos in God's holy house, you, Goodall', she cries out, while the congregation is 'almost fainting with shock'. 'How dare he stand there when he won't take the consequences of what he has done?' She is referring to the pregnancy of her daughter, the Annie of the story's title. Fanny, who is already unsure about whether she should go through with her coming marriage with Harry (it is supposed to take place in a fortnight), now has to deal with this new development. When Harry comes to her after the service has finished, he comments laconically that she has had 'a bit of an extra' and then, when challenged about the truth of the accusation made against him, says the coming baby might well be his, just as it might be that of several other young men in the town. He and Fanny go home to his mother's for Sunday tea, and there is some general conversation about the notorious moral shortcomings of the woman who has spoken out in church. Fanny is meanwhile mulling over what for her could accurately be called a life choice. When the time comes for Harry to return to the chapel for the evening service and Fanny is asked by Mrs Goodall whether she wants to go with him, her 'I'll stop with you tonight, mother,' makes clear in its final word what that decision is. The story is excellent in describing how most of us need to reconcile ourselves to limited possibilities.[8]

'Tickets Please!' is very different and more reflective of a temporary social situation. With the absence of so many men during the war, the local tram service which Lawrence would very probably have used occasionally while he was living in Mountain Cottage was largely staffed by young women. The story focuses on one of these women (also called Annie) and on a male ticket inspector, significantly named John Thomas, who has somehow avoided conscription and therefore finds himself with a numerous group of possible girlfriends. He 'walks out' with many of them, briefly enjoying himself with each before moving on to the next. Annie is among the rejected women and organizes a plot whereby a group isolates John Thomas in a waiting room, demands that he says which one of them he really prefers and, when he shows some resistance, attacks him like the women in *The Bacchae*, tearing his clothes and reducing him to submission. Although he then indicates that he prefers Annie, she is no longer attracted to someone she and her colleagues have succeeded in humiliating. The story could be seen as being, like *The Fox*, a comment by Lawrence on the way the war had led to women gaining powers previously held by men, although Annie's response to what she and her colleagues have done would be understandable without the unusual social circumstances.

The Lawrence who could compose these two excellent short stories was also the writer whose pieces on American authors in the *English Review* were rounded off in June 1919 with an essay called 'The Two Principles', one of the stranger texts he produced. What it attempts is a rewriting of Genesis in terms of an ancient, occult understanding that he insists is properly scientific: 'The ancient cosmic theories were exact, and apparently perfect. In them science and religion were in accord.' The 'two principles' with which he begins are fire and water, while operating between them is something he calls 'the creative mystery'. It is the attraction of these two mutual opposites that sets up a 'revolution in the universe' to the extent that 'the sun is formed by the impinging of the cosmic water on the cosmic fire, in the stress of opposition.' It is argued that water is H_2O, Lawrence writes, but

> In all our efforts to decompose water, we do but introduce fire into water ... and this introduction of naked fire into naked water produces hydrogen and oxygen, given the proper conditions of chemical procreation ... This is the alchemistic air. But from the conjunction of fire and water within the living plasm arose the first matter, the Prima Materia of a living body, which, in its dead state, is the alchemistic Earth.

What he wants to make clear is the 'true correspondence between the material cosmos and the living soul' and, in attempting to do so, he again views the human body in terms of a series of polarities between a top half which is spiritual and a bottom one which is sensual, or between a front which moves out towards the other and a back stiffened into isolation. Yet amid all these vertical and horizontal splits, Lawrence retains a belief he always had that 'in the blood we have our strongest self-knowledge, our most powerful dark conscience'.[9]

An adequate brief summary of 'The Two Principles' would be impossible. If one were wedded to Lawrence's own attachment to dualities – 'life depends on duality and polarity,' he writes in this essay – one could say that the two short stories represent a Lawrence

Rosalind Baynes, 1913.

wonderfully alive to and observant of day-to-day realities, while the essay reveals the mystical side of his nature. But that would be to misrepresent someone whose nature had far more sides than just two. It is nevertheless surprising how obstinately Lawrence continued to develop a whole world-view, despite his lack of expertise in certain specialist areas and sometimes in defiance of his usual pragmatism and common sense. Perhaps the most relevant commentary on his biological, metaphysical and psychological speculations is William Blake's famous remark: 'I must create a system or be enslaved by another man's.'[10]

That the war was coming to its end had not saved Lawrence from yet another medical examination, much more psychologically damaging than the three previous ones. What happened would later be described by him in the chapter of his Australian novel,

Kangaroo, that he called 'The Nightmare'. The examination took place not in faraway Cornwall but much closer to his home ground, in Derby, so it might have been that, on this occasion, the doctors knew who he was, which could have made their inspection of his body more humiliating than it might have been. This time, under the increasingly strict conscription regulations, he was graded fit for participation in the war effort, although only in a sedentary capacity. He began making enquiries among his influential friends for some kind of office job in a ministry, but the war had ended before he had to bother seriously.

The contact Lawrence had made with Douglas Goldring had other consequences apart from *Touch and Go*. It meant he could publish, in an obscure continental magazine of a left-wing persuasion, four very short essays on democracy which are more about his own idiosyncratic brand of metaphysics and psychology than they are about politics, and which all use Whitman as their starting point. But it also led to his being put in touch with a small New York publisher called Thomas Seltzer (Goldring happened to be his European agent). Seltzer was keen to publish anything by Lawrence and began making positive steps to secure a typescript of *Women in Love*. This meant that a year after Lawrence had left England, his novel would finally appear, although only in the United States (its English publication would have to wait until June 1921).

Having obtained her passport, Frieda left for Germany on 15 October 1919, with her husband due to follow about a month later. All Lawrence's talk of travelling on his own to America having been forgotten, they arranged to meet in Florence. Since April and his recovery from the flu, he had mostly been back in Hermitage, seeing again the two women who figure in *The Fox* but also someone he had known briefly before his retreat to Cornwall. This was Rosalind Baynes, who was living close by with her three children and was a daughter (like Connie in *Lady Chatterley's Lover*) of a well-known artist and member of the Royal Academy. She was in the process of divorcing her husband and, so as to be well out of the way while the possibly unpleasant formalities of this divorce were taking place, was looking to spend some time abroad, perhaps in an Abruzzi village called Picinisco, where she had been offered accommodation by an Italian who had once been one of her father's male models. Lawrence and Baynes clearly liked each other, and by the time he left England on 14 November 1919 he had promised to visit Picinisco in order to check whether it would be suitable for Baynes and her children.

6
A Busy Time!

Because Lawrence had arranged to meet Frieda in Florence, that is where he began making his way in November 1919. The one important contact he had there was the novelist and travel writer Norman Douglas, who had been a sub-editor of the *English Review* before the war. About to be charged with the sexual assault of two young boys, Douglas had been forced to live abroad and became a dominant presence among a group in Florence, most members of which were gay. Fussing around him like some anxious mother hen, when Lawrence met up with Douglas, was a dapper, cosmopolitan figure with an American accent. Maurice Magnus would claim that his mother was the illegitimate offspring of the German kaiser, but he had been brought up in New York. For Lawrence, there was something theatrical in his manner – which would not be surprising, given that he had once been the manager of the famous American dancer Isadora Duncan, who had taken Europe by storm in the days before the war. Times were now much harder for Magnus, who was trying to scrape a living through his writing and, like Douglas, was always hard up, yet the two men shared an attitude to financial matters quite unlike Lawrence's. The idea of adapting expenses to means was foreign to them, and they did their best to retain certain aspects of an upper-class lifestyle even when the financial resources for sustaining it were not easily available.

All three men stayed in the same Florence hotel, so that Lawrence was able to observe the contrast between Magnus's room – clean, full of tasteful trinkets and lightly perfumed – and that of Douglas, where they usually met to drink whisky. It did not

Norman Douglas, 1942, quarter-plate film negative.

help mitigate the sense of disorder in the latter that Douglas had an objection to ever opening his window. At one moment, Magnus startled Lawrence by complimenting him on the colour of his hair and asking whether it was dyed. Both men were impressively knowledgeable in certain areas and full of interesting conversation, so that Lawrence was able to spend the time pleasantly while he was waiting for Frieda to turn up. He must already have been familiar with Douglas's line in jovial, outspoken bawdy talk interspersed with genuine scholarly information, but Magnus was the kind of person he had never met before, and he was clearly fascinated. One reason for saying this is that Magnus was a Catholic convert and was about to spend a few weeks in the famous monastery at Monte

Cassino, 120 kilometres (75 mi.) or so southeast of Rome, so as to pursue his ambition of becoming a monk, and Lawrence must have more or less agreed to visit him there.

For the moment, however, he headed south with Frieda towards Capri, where he had other contacts. On their way, they took in Picinisco, the village in Abruzzo where the house Rosalind Baynes had asked him to check out was located. The journey was arduous, and when the Lawrences – who were used to roughing it – arrived in Picinisco, they found the conditions impossibly primitive. It was December and very cold, so it was immediately clear to them that, from the point of view of heating, sanitation and food preparation (cooking had to be done over an open fire), the house on offer would be totally unsuitable as even a temporary home for Baynes and her young children. They left as soon as they could, to avoid being snowed up, managing to arrive in Capri for the Christmas celebrations.

A beautiful island off the coast of Naples, Capri was a refuge in the years after the war for a large number of writers and artists, many of them English-speaking. Prominent among the latter was Compton Mackenzie, whom Lawrence had first met through the Cannans, and who had now become a highly successful author. They got on well together, so well that (according to Mackenzie) Lawrence became sufficiently intimate to communicate his anxieties about what he took to be his own failure to climax at the same time as Frieda in their lovemaking (a subject on which later, in *Lady Chatterley's Lover*, many different things would be said). Another former acquaintance the Lawrences met in Capri was Mary Cannan. Before marrying the novelist to whom she owed her current surname, she had been an actress and then the wife of J. M. Barrie (author of *Peter Pan*). But she had now divorced Gilbert Cannan after he had made her maid pregnant, suffered a mental crisis and shown less interest in her than his mistress.

Lawrence enjoyed Capri at first, but at the beginning of February 1920 he was once again ill with flu, and this was also the period of an episode that has perhaps brought him more discredit than any other. John Middleton Murry had moved in 1919 to a well-paid position as editor of a journal called *The Athenaeum* and had almost immediately asked Lawrence whether he had anything appropriate to submit. He seems to have then been sent several pieces, only one of which was accepted. The rejections upset Lawrence, and he swore to have nothing more to do with *The Athenaeum*, yet while he was in Florence, and after a warm exchange of letters with Mansfield, he relented and sent off a couple more contributions. The news that these were also refused, which he received in early February in Capri, sent him into a fury. He wrote to Murry denouncing him as a 'dirty little worm', but since the correspondence he received had been forwarded to him from Ospedaletti – a town on the Italian Riviera where Mansfield had been recuperating from TB, and where Murry would visit her when he was not busy in London – he assumed that whatever decisions had been taken about his writings were the responsibility of both of them. 'I loathe you,' he apparently told Mansfield. 'You revolt me stewing in your consumption. The Italians were quite right to have nothing to do with you.' The notepaper on which Lawrence is presumed to have written these cruel words no longer exists, so what we have instead is Mansfield's report to Murry, in a letter, as to what they were. She may have been exaggerating or joining together phrases to heighten their effect, yet there is no reason to think she made them up entirely or that, in one of his fits of anger, Lawrence was not capable of writing either them or words which were very similar. The remark about the Italians having nothing to do with Mansfield probably refers to what she or Murry had told him about hotels that would not accept clients suspected of having TB (a problem Lawrence himself would run into later).[1]

When he had first heard that Mansfield had been diagnosed some years earlier with TB, Lawrence was devastated. One of the letters he sent her afterwards was written in December 1918, after he had visited a childhood friend in Eastwood who also had tuberculosis and was just about to die. 'Be damned and be blasted everything, and let the bloody world come to its end,' he wrote. 'But one does not die. Jamais.'[2] This is that extreme belief in what Freud calls the omnipotence of thoughts, which Compton Mackenzie appears to have remembered Lawrence manifesting in Capri, since he has a character in one of his novels who is clearly based on him banging a stick against a wall there and declaring shrilly, 'I won't have another war.'³

Mark Kinkead-Weekes has conjectured that one of the pieces Murry rejected for *The Athenaeum* could have come from the six short essays Lawrence had completed by January 1920 for a book he called *Psychoanalysis and the Unconscious*.⁴ Since these ostensibly dealt with Carl Jung as well as Freud, he notes that Lawrence would have been especially upset by the rejection because it was a topic in which he had assumed, from previous contacts, that Mansfield showed a keen interest. Certainly, the Jungian influence is evident at the beginning of these essays, because it is there that Lawrence adopts the same tactic Jung had employed in combatting Freud's notions of infantile sexuality. That is to say Lawrence also argues that whatever sexual feelings from very early childhood an analyst may dredge up do not really belong there but are being projected back into the early years from later experience. They were never part, that is, of what he chooses to call the '*pristine* unconscious' (my italics), an entity it is the business of his six essays to describe. His explanations are reasonably lucid, even if they still focus on the two great nerve centres, or *chakras*, on the front of the body, in the breast and solar plexus, and the two corresponding ones in the lumbar region and thorax at the back. He saw the first two as operating in a sympathetic, merging or incorporating mode while the others represent repulsion or a willed retreat into selfhood. In Lawrence's view, it is the way these interact with the outside world, in both its human and non-human forms, which determines how a baby develops.

It is questionable how much of the accurate scientific knowledge Lawrence claims for his account is valid but there are certainly – in what are on the whole lucid, soberly written essays – hints of an anti-rationalism which will reveal itself more strongly later. At one point, for example, Lawrence casually remarks that 'the fixed and stable universe of law and matter . . . would wear out and disintegrate if it did not rest and find renewal in the quick centre of creative life in individual creatures'; at another he insists that any new human life is entirely causeless, so that 'the nature of the infant does not follow from the nature of its parents . . . cause-and-effect will not explain even the individuality of a single dandelion . . . individuality appears in defiance of all scientific law, in defiance even of reason.'[5]

Once he had sent his essays off to America and recovered from his flu, Lawrence was free to redeem the half-promise he had made to visit Magnus in the monastery at Monte Cassino, even though it meant a long and tiresome journey as well as more expenditure. He had already received a letter from him that hinted at financial difficulty and responded by sending £5, so he could hardly have been surprised to discover, once he was in the monastery, that one of Magnus's reasons for being there was to escape his creditors. The account Lawrence later wrote of Monte Cassino – perched on a hill, with an almost medieval farm life slowly going on around while the (then only forty) monks flitted through the ice-cold rooms of the huge building – is very fine. He could see immediately that the worldly Magnus, who talked of soon beginning his training as a monk, would never be happy there and told him so. Although Lawrence was currently quite well off, partly through having received advances from the United States for the imminent

Monte Cassino, the post-war rebuilt abbey.

publication of *Women in Love*, he did not feel in a position to lend any more money, but he began helping Magnus to find publishers for his writings. There were travel sketches but above all a memoir of the time Magnus had spent – amazingly enough – in the French Foreign Legion at the beginning of the First World War. Lawrence sensed that this text was marketable and sent off a few feelers on Magnus's behalf, although leaving his host still anxious about how he was going to deal with his more immediate needs.

Less than a week after his return from Monte Cassino, Lawrence decided that he had had enough of Capri and set off south to discover somewhere else he might settle. He had left Frieda behind in the company of Mary Cannan (who was also looking for a new location) and was accompanied by the novelist Francis Brett Young and his wife. After numerous disappointments, the party arrived in Taormina on the east coast of Sicily, where Lawrence found just what he was looking for in a house called Fontana Vecchia, set on a hill in the outskirts of the town. He immediately called for Frieda and Cannan to join him, knowing that, because Taormina was a tourist town, it had hotels where Mary could stay and enjoy the levels of comfort she expected.

Once he was settled with Frieda in Fontana Vecchia, Lawrence set to work again, this time on a novel. The origins of *The Lost Girl* were pre-war, in that story he had begun about a young woman's escape from her provincial background. This was inspired by the daughter of an Eastwood family called the Cullens, well known for having suffered a precipitous decline in social status thanks to the father's over-ambitious business ventures. In the novel, James Houghton has inherited a prosperous drapery store but overreaches himself by buying in ultra-fashionable stock which the local population fail to appreciate, finding it both too fancy and too expensive. The way Lawrence describes this first catastrophe is new and indicative of a wholly fresh approach to his own social origins. With a remarkable display of detailed knowledge of women's fashion, he nimbly satirizes James's misguided attempts to (as he himself might have put it) set pearls before swine. It makes for an enjoyable read, as does Lawrence's later account of how the disappointed James then

Fontana Vecchia, the Lawrences' home in Taormina.

moves on to try to repair his fortunes with brickmaking, a small open-cast mine which produces cheap but poor-burning coal and finally a cinema in which flickering, badly projected films are interspersed with variety acts that have failed to find anything better elsewhere. The chapter which describes the opening night of this final enterprise is one of the best examples of Lawrence's sustained comic writing.

So that James can make at least some headway in a field where he has no previous experience, he is shown taking on a strutting, dapper manager with an American accent called Mr May (a character clearly based on Maurice Magnus). One of the variety acts he hires is a troupe that enacts 'red Indian' scenarios of the type Lawrence must have seen in his childhood. It consists of four men, three of whom are Swiss and one Italian, as well as a world-wise French woman, who is in overall charge and dances the crucial female roles. This troupe calls itself the Natcha-Kee-Tawara, and James's daughter Alvina, the 'lost girl' of the novel's title, will eventually find herself playing the piano for them. Well before that, however, she has tried to secure some better kind of independence by training as a nurse, despite the disapproval of her family; on her return to Woodhouse (as Lawrence calls Eastwood in this novel), she has sunk back to waiting for some eligible bachelor to come along. When her father dies, it turns out that all the family money has been squandered and that any extra lustre which might have made Alvina more of a catch to the very few young men with backgrounds similar to hers no longer exists. She is an example of a problem about which there was a good deal of public discussion in the years leading up to the First World War and which that conflict greatly exacerbated: what to do about the thousands of middle-class women for whom there were just not enough suitable partners to go around.

Lawrence takes care to dramatize, very effectively, the unappealing nature of the one or two men who pay Alvina court before and after her father's death, and to show how she is faced with a typically Lawrentian dilemma of whether to follow the dictates of her mind and upbringing or lose caste entirely by acting on what her body tells her about her physical attraction to Ciccio, the uneducated Italian who is a member of the Natcha-Kee-Tawara. The description of how Alvina eventually comes to take this latter course includes two unpleasant scenes in which Ciccio forces her to have sex with him and is the opposite of romantic.[6] On the outbreak of the First World War, he takes her back to his home village in Italy, which is closely modelled by Lawrence on Picinisco. The material conditions she has to endure are therefore exceptionally harsh and, when Italy enters the war and Ciccio is called up, she is left pregnant and abandoned in a totally alien environment.

In rewriting *The Lost Girl*, Lawrence intended to produce a popular novel that would sell. To some extent he was successful: this was the only book of his to win a literary prize, and the vast bulk of it is a highly entertaining satirical account of middle-class life in a provincial Midlands town. But it would not be a novel by Lawrence without its theme of the body trumping the mind. Its initial inspiration might well have been Arnold Bennett's *Anna of the Five Towns*, and when he was reading that novel in Gargnano he had complained about its resignation and hopelessness.[7] Yet the conclusion of *The Lost Girl* is hardly a triumph of optimism. As is the case for so many Lawrentian heroes or heroines who make what his texts tell us is the right choice between the physical and mental, the personal consequences for Alvina are not brilliant.

Given that Lawrence appears to have discarded whatever he had written of *The Lost Girl* before the war and, as was his habit, started again from scratch, to have completed such a well-written work in a little more than two months was a remarkable achievement. He allowed himself few diversions, one of which was in any case forced on him at the beginning of May 1920, because it was then that Maurice Magnus unexpectedly turned up with a hunted look on his face. Learning that the police were on their way to Monte Cassino to interrogate him about cheques that had bounced, he had slipped out of the monastery before they arrived and made the long journey down to Taormina to throw himself on Lawrence's mercy. For someone who was himself never very well off, and had no more liking than any of us for emotional blackmail, it was an unpleasant situation which would have left Lawrence more sympathetic had Magnus not already booked himself into Taormina's more expensive hotel because, as he explained, he found the food at the other inedible (the more reasonable explanation he might have proffered is that it was only at expensive hotels where he had stayed before that he could check in without having to offer any money upfront).

It was a question of helping the fugitive out of the country and saving him from being arrested. Despite Frieda's objections, Lawrence agreed to settle Magnus's bill at the expensive hotel as long as he moved to cheaper lodgings and began helping him to cash a cheque which he had been sent from the United States. What Lawrence refused to do was to make the very long journey back to Monte Cassino in order to recover the belongings Magnus had been forced to leave behind there. After talking of a money-making scheme with contacts he had in Egypt, Magnus suddenly disappeared, leaving behind another bill, which Lawrence was happy enough to settle as the price of getting rid of him. The American was no longer on his mind, therefore, when, with *The Lost Girl* now finished, Lawrence accepted an offer Mary Cannan had made to pay the passage for a week's trip to Malta at the end of May. Yet once she and the Lawrences were on the boat, there also was Magnus, and Lawrence must have seen quite a bit of him during his week's stay on the island. We know this from a letter Magnus sent to Douglas, in which he claimed that Lawrence had 'opened his "heart"(!) to me here accidentally' and said 'he was looking for bisexual types for *himself*.' He explained that Lawrence did not like Malta because he thought 'religion or something' prevented sexual expression, adding knowingly, 'I didn't elucidate him as I could have done even after a few days stay!'[8]

Magnus's account of Lawrence's conversation seems garbled, but there having been some talk of his bisexuality is likely enough and suggests that the two of them got on well enough once they were on British territory and Magnus had no immediate fear of arrest. By the time the Lawrence party left Malta he was settling in nicely, having made a couple of Maltese friends and arranged for the renting of a house. Lawrence was to hear nothing more of him until November,

Maurice Magnus (1876–1920), American travel writer and memoirist.

when the news came of an extradition order and of how, to avoid arrest, Magnus had poisoned himself. What made it a greater shock was Lawrence's assumption that, had he been willing to give Magnus more money, the suicide might never have happened. Partly to salve his own conscience, and partly to help compensate a Maltese from whom Magnus had borrowed money, he undertook to write a long introduction to the latter's *Memoirs of the Foreign Legion* so that it might have a better chance of being published. He was to describe this introduction as the best thing, 'as writing', he had ever done, and in its account of all his dealings with Magnus, from that first meeting in Florence to the last one in Malta, it is a compelling piece.[9] Lawrence does not disguise how detestable he finds those who tear at other people's heartstrings in order to exploit them, but he praises Magnus for being able to survive conditions, in the Foreign Legion especially, which he himself could not have endured – and he admires him for taking his own life rather than suffer the humiliation of arrest.

For people who feared the cold, Taormina was a good place to be in winter, but in the summer it could be intolerably hot. On top of this, Frieda, whose father had died during the war but whose mother was in a care home in Baden-Baden, was keen to get back to Germany. In late July and early August, the Lawrences made their way northwards to Milan, where they separated, with Lawrence going off on a walking tour around Lake Como with the daughter and son-in-law of his former landlord in Zennor, while Frieda headed for Germany. By September 1920, he was again in the Florence area, visiting friends and waiting for his wife to reappear.

One of the friends Lawrence visited was Rosalind Baynes. She had been living in a village outside Florence called San Gervasio, but after an explosion in a nearby ammunitions factory had blown out her villa's windows, she had moved a little further off to Fiesole. This meant that a deserted, if windowless, property was available for Lawrence to move into, which he very happily did (it was, after all, summer), taking with him the little Primus stove he had been using on his recent walking holiday. Nothing pleased him better than the freedom and independence of being able to camp in a large, empty house with a fine garden. For company, he could go into Florence or take the short walk up to Fiesole to see Baynes. It is as clear as these things can be that at some point the meeting between these two resulted in their sleeping together, and this is therefore the one clear indication we have of Lawrence having been unfaithful to Frieda.

The period was one in which he had gone back to writing poems, those which, when he collected them together, he would call *Birds, Beasts and Flowers*. The most famous poem in this remarkable collection, the one most anthologized, is called 'Snake', but that describes an encounter which took place in Taormina. To San Gervasio belong several poems about fruit trees that have a strong erotic flavour ('Fig' would be a good example); it is also the origin of six poems about the tortoises Lawrence happened to find in the garden there. The brilliantly observed and often humorous account of these strange creatures begins by celebrating the independence of the baby tortoise as it sets out on its life's journey, an 'invincible forerunner'. Then Lawrence notes the markings of a cross on the tortoise shell which means that it cannot always enjoy its independence but is 'crucified into sex', doomed to seek out a relationship. The poems describe this seeking out and, in the final one ('Tortoise Shout'), Lawrence notes how surprised he is to find that the smaller, male tortoise – which he had thought of as voiceless and which is spreadeagled on the back of the much larger female – lets out an unnerving scream at the moment of coition. This is an indication of

> The cross,
> The wheel on which our silence first is broken,
> Sex, which breaks up our integrity, our single inviolability, our deep silence
> Tearing a cry from us.[10]

That is not a cheerful view of sexual intercourse, and although Baynes's account of sleeping with Lawrence suggests an experience that was altogether relaxed and pleasant, it may be that it excited feelings in him which he found uncomfortable.

Having recuperated Frieda, Lawrence was back in Sicily by October 1920. In *The Lost Girl* he had developed a distanced, humorous approach to his own social background, and now, in a new novel he called *Mr Noon*, he took this even further and gave a burlesque account of the sexual mores of Eastwood, basing it initially on the misfortunes of his old friend George Neville, who had made a local girl pregnant and been obliged to marry her. This was a topic his mother had made him feel was of fearful significance – one moment of self-abandon and a young man's life could be blighted for ever (not to mention a young woman's) – but now he treated it in a comic, carefree manner. Having then allowed his eponymous hero to just about escape being trapped in Woodhouse (the same name for his hometown he had adopted in *The Lost Girl*) in what he called Part One of this novel, he transformed him into someone very like himself in a second part as he recounted, in a similar wry, amused manner, his own early involvement with Frieda and some of his adventures with her in Germany. After an attempt to sum up the influence Otto Gross had had on his wife, this second instalment reaches the moment when Noon and Johanna (as Lawrence calls Frieda) cross the Alps into Italy on foot. As *Aaron's Rod* had on several occasions, the narrative then stalled, but in contrast to that novel, Lawrence never subsequently found any reason for starting this one up again.

He was a ferociously hard worker who needed diversions. In January 1921, he decided to take a short trip to Sardinia, although it was entirely characteristic that the upshot should then be another book. *Sea and Sardinia* is the most truly authentic travel book Lawrence ever wrote, as well as being a work often recommended as an introduction to his writing, since it shows him at his most effortlessly impressive and relaxed. Cast in the form of a diary, it conveys a vivid impression of being written on the hoof, whereas what it in fact demonstrates is Lawrence's amazing power of visual recall. Characteristic of its tone is that, in its descriptions of the numerous practical mishaps of their short journey to Sardinia, Frieda should affectionately be referred to as the 'q-b' (queen bee), and Lawrence manifests a strong sense of how eccentric a couple the two of them must have seemed to the Sardinians, carrying their own tea-making equipment and with a bedraggled appearance quite unexpected in foreign tourists. There are parts of the island which impress Lawrence, but he had gone there in the hope of discovering a culture more authentically primitive than the one he already knew in Sicily, and on the whole what he found was, he felt, a land that was primitive in the wrong way (especially in its toilet arrangements). Much later, in a book review, he would write, 'We travel, perhaps, with a secret and absurd hope of setting foot on the Hesperides . . . [But] the hope is always defeated. There is no Garden of Eden, and the Hesperides never were.'[11]

In April, the Lawrences headed north again, rather earlier than they had the year before. They called in on Capri and met for the first time a couple called the Brewsters, who came from the United States but were living in almost permanent exile in Europe with their young daughter. A bond was established immediately when it turned out that Earl and Achsah Brewster had spent their honeymoon in Fontana Vecchia, and Lawrence had interesting discussions with Earl about the Buddhist creed he had adopted. From there they pressed on towards Baden-Baden, settling not in the town itself but in a cheap hotel in Ebersteinburg, an outlying village. It was there that Lawrence again, and for the final time, picked up the much-interrupted *Aaron's Rod*.

He had moved this novel on by making his hero's movements his own, taking him after the war to Florence and a meeting with the Norman-Douglas circle, yet *Aaron's Rod* is unique in having two alter egos rather than just one. The flute-playing Aaron is someone of working-class origins who abandons his roots and the responsibilities he has in his local community. When he falls ill, a man called Lilly looks after him, partly by massaging – in a strange, obscurely homoerotic fashion – all his lower body with oil. Although Lilly has the same social background as Aaron, he is now a writer, already well established in the intellectual community and willing to guide Aaron, to act as his spiritual leader, as long as he accepts him as his moral and intellectual superior, someone qualified to act in that role. In the finale, after there has been a terrorist explosion in a Florence café and Aaron's flute has been destroyed, whether or not he will accept Lilly's leadership has not been finally resolved.

Working with two alter egos caused Lawrence some problems. In an episode where Aaron is on his way to Florence, he reflects at length on what has gone wrong with his marriage and on the 'diabolical female will' of his wife, the conviction 'as firm as steel, that she as woman, was the centre of creation ... the great source of life and being, and also of culture'. The trouble has been that Aaron himself possesses 'the arrogance of the self-unyielding male'. After several paragraphs of reflections on these matters, Lawrence becomes aware that they are not especially appropriate for a man like Aaron (although they would suit Lilly very well). 'Thoughts something in this manner' ran through Aaron's mind, he writes, although 'he could not have fired it all off at any listener, as these pages are fired off at any chance reader'. A little later, Lawrence addresses those readers directly and tells them not to worry that his hero might seem not 'half clever enough to think all these smart things', concluding, 'You are quite right, he wasn't, yet it all resolved in him as I say, and it is for you to prove that it didn't.'[12] This final off-the-cuff remark is an indication of Lawrence's inclination to play fast and loose with the novel form in *Aaron's Rod*, as indeed he had been doing in *Mr Noon*, although in both cases he could take some cover under the notion of the picaresque, with its plots entirely dependent on the adventures of a central character and its periodic disruptions of a realist framework with addresses to the reader.

There are so many different aspects to Lawrence's literary personality that trying to give a brief account of them all can become bewildering, and in this short period especially, he produced so much that it is difficult to avoid giving the reader an impression of just one damned thing after another. In Ebersteinburg, he insisted on writing a much more detailed expansion of his ideas on psychoanalysis and the unconscious, even though his first brief sketch had been received unfavourably when it had appeared in the United States (the effect of criticism on Lawrence was usually to make him more pugnacious and determined). This time, he began by directly contesting a claim one of his critics had assumed to be Freud's: that all human action can eventually be traced back to a sexual motivation. While admitting that sex was very important in life and congratulating Freud for having made that so clear, Lawrence credited it as only half of life's motivating force, claiming that the other half came from a religious or creative urge, the desire (of men in particular!) to achieve something new in the world.

Aware of how little sympathy his ideas were likely to receive, Lawrence adopted a bantering tone in this new book and called it first a 'harlequinade' and then a 'fantasia' of the unconscious. A good example of its general manner would be the way he now expresses what had been Ursula Brangwen's conviction, in the laboratory of her university, that it is impossible to contemplate an organism under the microscope without presupposing some initial creative mystery or life force – what in *Fantasia of the Unconscious* Lawrence is now quite willing to call a soul.[13] Not to do so, he claims, would be like taking a cart, rubbing it all over with oil and

D. H. Lawrence's passport photo, 1921.

expecting suddenly to see a horse 'panting between the shafts'.[14] This is a metaphor rather than an argument, but in an area where faith is always likely to count more than logic.

From Ebersteinburg, the Lawrences moved to the beautiful Austrian resort of Zell am See, invited there by Frieda's younger sister, who lived in a world of fashion and elegance. This meant daily bathing in the lake and periodic trips to the surrounding mountains. It was partly the sophistication of this milieu that was later to prompt Lawrence to write *The Captain's Doll*, an excellent novella about an artist called Hannele, who has been the mistress of a Captain Hepburn and fashioned a doll of him widely regarded as breathtakingly lifelike. The story concerns the struggle Hepburn has to persuade Hannele to accept his male dominance, and it is a sign of her possible eventual acquiescence that she agrees to destroy her beautiful doll. The light, semi-comic tone of this novella makes it one of the best things Lawrence wrote, and when it appeared together with two others – *The Fox* and *The Ladybird*, both having been radically altered from earlier versions – the resulting volume was a clearer proof of what an accomplished writer Lawrence was than *Aaron's Rod* or the unfinished *Mr Noon*, even if it contained what for many would be disturbing implications. In the revised *The Fox*, for example, the relationship of the two young women trying to run the farm is more clearly seen as lesbian and, when the returning soldier breaks it up, he does so by making sure that a tree he is cutting down kills one of them.

Frieda was very happy in Zell am See, but Lawrence, much as he liked his sister-in-law, grew tired of being surrounded by in-laws and persuaded his wife to return with him to the relative isolation of Fontana Vecchia. It was there, in November 1921, that he received a crucial letter. The sender was a rich American patroness of the arts named, at this point, Mabel Dodge Sterne, the past and future alterations in her name corresponding with changes of husband. She was developing an interest in what she called Indian culture and had bought a house in Taos, New Mexico, with dependencies where she could lodge visiting writers or artists. Having read an extract of *Sea and Sardinia* in an American journal, she had concluded that Lawrence was just the man to write about Taos and bring it to worldwide attention. This offer of what would be free accommodation, combined with a fascination Lawrence had long had for Native American culture, made him take a keen interest in Sterne's offer. After all, he had been planning to escape Europe and make his way to the United States since 1916, and here was a solution which would take him straight to a part of the country that intrigued him far more than its industrialized northeast.

He hesitated nevertheless, worried that he might find himself in some pretentious artists' colony, and the object of a condescending patronage. While he was mulling over the offer, he was also thinking about an invitation that had been renewed by the Brewsters to visit them during their projected stay in Sri Lanka and take a look at Buddhism on one of its native grounds. What he then decided was that he and Frieda would sail to the East first, and after six months or so move on to the United States from there. On 26 February 1922, therefore, the two of them were on a passenger boat which set sail from Naples, heading for Colombo. The tickets cost more than £70 each, which appalled Lawrence, but he must have felt comforted by the news that the James Tait Black Memorial Prize, which had recently been awarded to *The Lost Girl*, was worth £100.

7
A Wider World

One of the aspects of his wife's character Lawrence seems to have appreciated is that she could be perfectly happy lazing around. He himself was different and took care to have with him on the *Osterley*, as the boat they took was called, a work by the well-known Sicilian novelist Giovanni Verga, which he had decided to translate (after his version of *Mastro-don Guesualdo* had appeared, he would also translate and publish Verga's *Little Novels of Sicily*). Even though the Lawrences were travelling second class, both the accommodation and food on the *Osterley* were excellent, and Lawrence enjoyed the company of his fellow travellers, who were mostly Australian. So agreeable did he find them that the previously vague thoughts he had entertained about stopping in Australia after Ceylon were considerably strengthened.

Arriving in Colombo on 13 March 1922, they were met by the Brewsters, who took them to a rented bungalow in Kandy, large enough for all four. It was close to a famous temple which housed a relic of the Buddha (his supposed tooth) and where Brewster was studying Buddhist texts. The Lawrences' arrival roughly coincided with a version of a religious event known as a Perahera which was being put on specially for the visit of Edward, Prince of Wales. Lawrence gave an account of this ceremony in a poem called 'Elephant', making clear how disappointed he was that Edward appeared unable to assert the natural leadership in which he himself had become very interested at this juncture.

Lawrence had high hopes of staying in Sri Lanka for a few months and writing about the country and its culture, but these were soon dashed by the effects on his health of the hot and humid climate. He would say afterwards that he had never felt 'so sick in [his] life' as he did 'in Ceylon'.[1] By 24 April 1923, he and Frieda were on a boat heading for Perth and once again enjoying the company of Australians. After they had docked, one of these new acquaintances recommended a boarding house outside the city which was run by an Englishwoman called Mollie Skinner. During the recent war, she had been a nurse in India as a member of the Voluntary Aid Detachment, and had published a book based on her experiences. She had also written a historical novel, which Lawrence saw enough of to be convinced she had talent, but he urged her to profit more from her local Australian knowledge and write about the early days of Western Australia, perhaps using her brother Jack, a war veteran, as a hero. When she later, having taken his advice, sent what she had written to him while he was living in the United States, he suggested that her novel was only likely to find its way into print if he rewrote it. Even before securing her agreement, this is what he began doing, although *The Boy in the Bush* was unlike *The Trespasser* insofar as its title page made clear it was a collaboration.

From Perth, the Lawrences sailed around the Australian coast to Sydney, the natural jumping-off point, in Lawrence's view, for the United States. But he wasn't ready to jump just yet, and after only a day or two, he found a house to rent in Thirroul, 64 kilometres (40 mi.) south of Sydney, on the New South Wales coast, where he could settle down to write. It was cheap because, with Australia moving into winter at the end of May, the holiday season was over. With a sardonic Australian flavour Lawrence came to appreciate, the house was called Wyewurk; in the long novel Lawrence would produce after less than three months in Wyewurk, he would have the wife of his alter ego make fun of him for assuming that the name of the house which they are about to rent, Torestin, was a foreign word and not three short English ones stuck together.

Lawrence called the novel he wrote *Kangaroo*, and it is in certain respects a travel book, often at its best as such. That is to say that incidental to its main action are vivid evocations of what is known in Australia as 'the bush' and of the Pacific seashore where Lawrence was then living. It also shrewdly registers, initially with some discomfort, the more egalitarian nature of interpersonal relations in Australia, much less class-bound than in England. Yet for the core of his novel Lawrence turned to politics. In his last months in Italy, he could not but be aware of the growing tensions between Left and Right in that country, as elsewhere in Europe. These would come to a head in October 1922, when Mussolini's notorious March on Rome would result in his becoming the first fascist to take over a European country (long before Hitler). In many ways, Lawrence seems to have transferred the conflict between Italian communists and fascists into an Australian context, although the same division certainly existed there and he may have spoken to Australians about various political organizations similar to those in Europe, and even had contact with one or two of their members.

Richard Lovatt Somers, as the chief male character in *Kangaroo* is called, is a writer who has come to Australia because he feels that everything is 'played out, finished' in Europe, and in no other of Lawrence's novels is there a more obvious substitute for himself. Attributed to Somers, for example, are those short essays on democracy, each with a starting point in Whitman, that Douglas Goldring had arranged for Lawrence himself to publish, while his memory of humiliating experiences in England during the war are easily identifiable as his creator's own. In what is perhaps an overestimation by Lawrence of his own value to others, Somers is courted by figures from both the Australian Left and Right, but, despite what is identified as his working-class background, he is attracted much less by the communist trade-union leader than by a charismatic Jewish lawyer who heads the alternative right-wing movement, largely made up of veterans from the war. Ben Cooley, known by his followers as 'Kangaroo', is a large, physically imposing figure given to clasping Somers to his ample chest and telling him how much he loves him. He espouses that 'love of comrades' Lawrence had previously written about in one of his essays on Whitman. 'The next belief', he had said then, 'is to be a hot belief of men in each other, a culminating belief, culminating in a final leader and hero.' 'The one comrade is leader,' he had added, 'the other the passionate believer and answerer . . . It is a relationship in perfect leadership and liege love.'[2] This is the union that Lilly had wanted Aaron to accept in *Aaron's Rod*, and it is what Kangaroo now demands of Somers, although in a far more homoerotic fashion as he presses his much larger body against the writer's.

Somers sees his own value to the organizations who want to recruit him, not so much as a writer but as someone who paves the way to the future by being able to hear and interpret the messages that come from below, from the 'dark gods'. This prophet-like capacity is something his creator felt he shared, but – as Jesus noted – a prophet fails to be honoured not only in his own country but in his own household. In a chapter of *Kangaroo* entitled 'Harriet and Lovat at Sea in Marriage', Lawrence describes the unavailing efforts of Somers to persuade his wife that he ought to take the leading role in their relationship. Their marriage is at a point where the 'perfect love' that characterized their early years has gone and they now have to choose between either companionship or Harriet's acceptance of her husband's dominance (someone has to be captain of their ship). Lawrence had both declared and dramatized many times before his belief that men should lead the way forward and their wives follow, but it is evident that he had difficulty in making Frieda share this belief, as is made clear by the way, in *Kangaroo*, Harriet responds to Somers's suggestions:

> Him, a lord and master! Why, he was not really lord of his own bread and butter, next year they might both be starving. And he was not even master of himself, with his ungovernable furies and his uncritical intimacies with people . . .
>
> All he could do was try to come it over her with this revolution rubbish and a stunt of 'male' activity. If it were even real![3]

As in *Women in Love*, Lawrence is capable of looking at the beliefs and ambitions of his male protagonists from a sceptical point of view and exposing them to criticism, but that does not mean that they are ready to abandon them (any more than he was).

Aaron's Rod had ended, or been brought to an end, by a terrorist incident in Florence, and *Kangaroo* similarly concludes with a political riot in which Kangaroo is shot. It is not long afterwards that Somers and Harriet prepare to leave Australia, just as the Lawrences were then doing. They took a boat from Sydney Harbour on 11 August 1922, calling in on New Zealand and the South Sea islands on their way to the west coast of America. From Mansfield's birthplace of Wellington, Lawrence sent her a postcard bearing the single word 'riccordi' (a minor gesture of reconciliation). Commenting – in a letter to Mary Cannan at the end of August – on Tahiti and other South Sea islands, of which he had taken such a favourable impression from Melville's writing, he described travelling as 'a splendid lesson in disillusion – chiefly that'.[4]

When the Lawrences landed in San Francisco on 4 September, they were broke, which was not surprising given what all their sea journeys had cost. The good news was that Mabel Dodge, now divorced from Sterne, had sent them train tickets to Lamy in New Mexico, where, she explained, they would be picked up and taken to Taos; even better was a note from Lawrence's American agent, Robert Mountsier, to say that *The Captain's Doll* had been sold to a magazine for $1,000. Even with the dollar at three or four to the pound, this was a tidy sum, and it became clear that there would be more money in the offing when Lawrence heard that his U.S. publisher, Thomas Seltzer, had been prosecuted for his edition of *Women in Love* and that the case had just recently been dismissed. The result was that the edition of the novel sold out, and Seltzer was obliged to print more copies. Here was an early lesson on the relation between notoriety and commercial success, which Lawrence could hardly forget.

The Lawrences found Mabel waiting for them at Lamy in a car driven by her Native American lover, Tony Luhan. Mechanical troubles on the road meant that when they arrived in Santa Fe, it was too late to press on to Taos. She turned for help to an old friend called Witter Bynner, who had a house there, which he shared with Willard Johnson, one of his former students in a poetry class he had taught at the University of California, Berkeley. Bynner was a well-established writer and, like most of Mabel's friends and associates, left wing, so there was plenty for the Lawrences to talk about when they spent the night there.

The delay in Santa Fe meant that Lawrence arrived in Taos on 11 September 1922, his 37th birthday. Mabel Dodge was (like Frieda) five years older than him and had a long and colourful history behind her. A rough equivalent in American terms of Lady Ottoline Morrell, she had already been the organizing spirit of several groups of avant-garde writers, artists and thinkers, and before the war had created a salon in Florence, in a house called the Villa Curonia, of which her home in Taos was something of an adobe replica. When the Lawrences dined there, it would be with a succession of interesting figures from the art or political world, and she organized for their benefit demonstrations of Native American dancing by young men from the nearby pueblo. Their own rent-free four-roomed cottage, which she had filled with local artefacts, was

Mabel Luhan, 1934.

D. H. Lawrence in Santa Fe, 1922.

only 180 metres (200 yd) away. Taken to several Native American ceremonies, Lawrence was at first disconcerted by the difference between what he saw and the notion of 'Red Indians' he had derived from the writing of James Fenimore Cooper, and it took him some time to adjust his thinking. The result was that he was perhaps not immediately the wholehearted supporter of the Native American cause that Mabel expected him to be, although he was quick to recognize and deplore efforts that the government were then making to suppress the local culture and force the inhabitants of the pueblos into the economic mainstream.

Apart from enrolling Lawrence in the group of those willing to defend and celebrate her causes, Mabel Dodge wanted him to write a novel based on her eventful life. This meant more one-to-one meetings than Frieda was willing to contemplate, and the enterprise quickly collapsed. Enough was achieved, however, for Lawrence to decide that he had identified in his hostess the same powerful will which he felt he had discovered in Lady Ottoline, and which he had gone on to dramatize in the conflict between Hermione Roddice and Rupert Birkin in *Women in Love*. There was no doubt that Mabel was a powerful as well as wealthy individual, used to getting her own way – later she would admit that her intention had indeed been to take Lawrence away from Frieda – but his criticism of her had a lot to do with the discomfort he felt in being so inescapably in her debt. He began exploring ways of removing himself from her sphere of influence, from 'Mabeltown' (as he put it), eventually finding a family of ranchers in the mountains, about 27 kilometres (17 mi.) from Taos, who had a cabin they were willing to rent. To move to the Del Monte ranch in the winter was full of practical difficulties, but Lawrence partly addressed them by inviting two impecunious young Danish painters, Knud Merrild and Kai Gøtzsche, who had recently arrived in Taos, to join the Lawrences in another cabin close by, for which Lawrence would pay the modest rent. Shortly before Christmas, and to Mabel's chagrin, this party of four moved off her estate.

During these months, the experience of actually being in America prompted Lawrence to revise quite substantially his *Studies*

Mabel Dodge's house in Taos.

in Classic American Literature before they were published in book form. Apart from adjusting his comments on Cooper and Native Americans, he cut out a good deal of the Theosophical thinking that had preoccupied him during the war years, not because he no longer believed in its precepts (the central male characters in his coming 'Mexican novel' are at one point full of an 'esoteric' jargon that would have made Madame Blavatsky proud), but rather because he felt it would not go down well with an American audience. It was perhaps with that supposed audience in mind that Lawrence also adopted a much more direct and colloquial form of address, a kind of telegraphese, with sentences reduced to single words, exclamation marks and slang terms. This certainly makes some of the studies livelier but can also on occasions deprive them of their coherence, the essay on Whitman being a good example.

It was about this time also that Lawrence responded to a request he received for some thoughts on the novel as an art form. While he was in Australia, he had become more aware of the shock *Ulysses* was causing in literary circles and imagined that, in his own free-wheeling attitude to the novel form in *Aaron's Rod* and *Kangaroo*, he was doing very similar things to James Joyce. When in New Mexico he managed to acquire a copy of *Ulysses*, he quickly became aware of how wrong he had been. In the essay that became 'The Future of the Novel', he denounced the works of Joyce, Marcel Proust and Dorothy Richardson for their self-consciousness and said that what interested him were novels that would indicate, as the current culture continued its inevitable decline, 'what feelings do we want to carry through into the next epoch'. Having suggested that the four gospels were really novels, and Plato's dialogues 'queer little' ones, he expressed his regret that fiction and philosophy had ever got separated. The future of the novel, he claimed, was 'to take the place of gospels, philosophies, and the present-day novel as we know it'.[5]

It began snowing almost as soon as the Lawrence party were settled in their cabins, and daily life became even tougher. At times they had to melt snow for water to wash, but Lawrence seems to have preferred these inconveniences to the comforts of life in Mabeltown. One valuable and enjoyable skill he and Frieda had acquired in Taos was to ride horses, and the always accommodating owner of the Del Monte ranch lent or rented them mounts to replace those Mabel Dodge had provided. That they could eat practically every night with the Danes did not make their new home too lonely – but, in any case, the approach of Christmas found them expecting visitors. There were, first of all, Thomas Seltzer and his wife Adèle. Both were fervent fans of Lawrence, and Adèle added to her appeal by being able to speak fluent German with Frieda. Less welcome was the visit of Lawrence's agent, Robert Mountsier, which followed immediately after. It was not so much the lack of room which meant they could not all come together but that a violent antipathy had developed between the two parties. Mountsier regarded Seltzer as a small-time publisher who was never likely to do Lawrence much good, and he badgered him to improve the contracts he offered and to be more efficient in fulfilling their conditions. Their relations had become so acrimonious that Seltzer suggested he could not carry on working with Mountsier anymore, but Lawrence's relationship with his agent went back a long time, and he must have been aware not only that he had done his best to promote his work but that many of his criticisms of Seltzer's inefficiencies were valid. What may have prompted Lawrence to resolve a difficult situation by sacking Mountsier was that the latter, in direct contrast to the Seltzers, had been distinctly unenthusiastic about his recent work, disliking *Aaron's Rod* and urging him not to continue his thinking about psychoanalysis and the unconscious into a second book. He also seems to have lacked the social instinct which allows people not to overstay their welcome. That is what he had done when he paid a visit to the Lawrences in Eberstinburg, and he did it again at Del Monte. Yet any discomfort Lawrence might have felt about choosing the Seltzers over Mountsier was a little alleviated by the indignation he felt when his now former agent charged him $300 for his journey back to New York. Could it really have cost that much, Lawrence asked?

By late March 1923, he was ready to be on the move again, this time for a trip down to Mexico. He hoped that the Danes would come too, but their plan had always been to travel on to California, and there was an exhibition of their work in Taos pending. Keen not to find himself and Frieda alone, Lawrence approached Bynner and Johnson, who said they would be glad to join in a Mexican trip. On their way south, the Lawrences passed through Santa Fe, but Bynner had some final arrangements to make before he could travel, so they agreed to meet up again in Mexico City in a few days' time.

This proved more complicated than initially envisaged, but before long the two couples were staying in the Monte Carlo Hotel in Mexico City, which Lawrence liked because it was inexpensive and run by Italians. They used it as a base for several trips, perhaps the most significant of which was to the pyramids at nearby Teotihuacán. It was there that Lawrence saw the recently excavated images of the pre-Aztec god Quetzalcoatl, the 'feathered serpent'. These, and other signs of Mexican religion which pre-dated the imposition on the country of Catholicism by the Spanish, would stimulate him to write a novel in which he imagined a whole new political system for Mexico, a theocracy based on a former pantheon of indigenous gods.

For the moment, however, he was still not sure if he wanted to stay in Mexico: there were some aspects of life there that repelled him, including the bullfight he attended with Johnson and Bynner in their first days. He was also under some pressure from Frieda, keen to return to Europe to see her mother and also her children, who were reaching an age when their father's legal measures to ensure they remained out of contact with their mother no longer had any force. Nothing could be more reasonable than that she should want to be reunited with them, but it was a wish which tended to infuriate her husband. Bynner remembered how once, when she was looking at some photographs in which they figured, Lawrence called her a 'sniffling bitch', snatched them from her and tore them into bits. He, Johnson and the Danes all record episodes like this of uncontrollable rage in Lawrence – often, although not always, directed at Frieda. In Mexico City, his temper seems to have been unusually volatile as he struggled to decide whether he should go or stay, and if he stayed, where that should be. The solution came indirectly through a young woman called Idella Purnell, whose American father had married a Mexican and now lived in Guadalajara, some 480 kilometres (300 mi.) to the west of Mexico City. She had been with Johnson in the same poetry class Bynner taught at Berkeley, and now ran a small poetry magazine called *Palms* while working in the u.s. consulate. The two men had always planned to visit her, and when they did so, Lawrence went with them in a final, somewhat desperate attempt to see whether there was anywhere in Mexico he felt he could settle. Quite close to Guadalajara was a lakeside resort called Chapala, which took his fancy. He immediately began making arrangements for renting a house there and telegraphed to Frieda to join him. 'He will be writing again there,' Bynner reports Frieda saying. 'He will be happier.'[6]

There are no obvious prototypes in real life for the two friends who, in Lawrence's new novel (initially called *Quetzalcoatl* and later revised to *The Plumed Serpent*), initiate the religion of Quetzalcoatl in Chapala. The warm bond of fellowship they establish is ideal, according to his more recent prescriptions, in that Cipriano has no difficulty in acknowledging Ramón's superiority and identifying himself as his follower. Not only do they want to revive the old gods, but they feel the need, if their new regime is going to be accepted, to embody them: Ramón as Quetzalcoatl and Cipriano as Huitzilopochtli, the old Aztec god of war. In one of the novel's more effective episodes, the Christian icons are removed from the church in Chapala so that they can be replaced with images of indigenous deities. Lawrence had repeatedly said the old Christian epoch was coming to an end (had not all its talk of Whitmanesque sympathy and love culminated in the First World War?), but he had never been very informative on what would replace it. Now he attempted to imagine something quite new, even if that meant going back to something very old.

Since the regime Ramón and Cipriano seek to establish is basically feudal, it seems entirely contrary to the Bolshevism which, with Bynner's warm approval, was active in Mexico at the time. Having participated in at least one left-wing rally in Mexico City, he and Johnson had settled with the Lawrences in Chapala for a while, but in the local hotel rather than a rented house. Their political discussions must have been frequent, with Lawrence insisting that Bolshevism was an imposition on Mexico from abroad, just as the Catholic Church had been. Despite some gestures along the lines of *reculer pour mieux sauter* – Gudrun Brangwen's explanation for returning to her hometown in *Women in Love* – it is difficult to imagine how Lawrence could have thought that the regime he describes Ramón and Cipriano initiating was anything other than retrogressive. At least, he might have argued, his descriptions of it were neither nostalgic nor sentimental. In a well-written scene, a group of locals attack Ramón's hacienda, and his life is only saved by the novel's heroine, Kate Leslie, shooting at one of them. Several of the attackers are arrested and, in an episode made more chilling when Lawrence later revised *Quetzalcoatl* into *The Plumed Serpent*, executed by Cipriano himself in public. One of the effects of the New Mexican and Mexican landscape on Lawrence was to rid him of any vestiges of the Romantic idea that nature was essentially benign. He would claim that he preferred to be aware of its harsher aspects, because at least he then felt he was in contact with what

Frieda Lawrence in Chapala, Mexico, 1923.

was real. Violence and killing were part of those essentials of nature in its human as well as all its other manifestations, which not only legitimized his own rages, but helped to provide a bedrock for thinking about the future that was more reliable than the 'love and sympathy' model.

Many of the most impressive passages in *Quetzalcoatl* describe the landscape around Lake Chapala, so that, like *Kangaroo*, it often seems to function best as a travel book. When Lawrence rented his house, he was obliged to take with it a family of Mexican servants, who provided him with insights into how ordinary Mexicans lived and gave him copy for his novel. The wonder, admiration and exasperation that the servants excite in Kate Leslie are also one of *Quetzalcoatl*'s stronger features. She is a widowed Irishwoman of Frieda's age, who frequently feels she might want to go back to Europe to see her mother and children. For reasons that are not easy to understand, Cipriano is desperate for her to remain in Mexico as his wife, but he is Indian, and she is not at all sure she approves of interracial marriage. While they were still in Mexico, news came to the Lawrences that Mabel Dodge had married Tony Luhan. It created in both of them a far-from-creditable shock and a response that can only be described as racist given that Tony was a Native American chief of the Taos pueblo. By the time Lawrence came to revise his novel, his feelings had changed, and Kate does indeed marry Cipriano – but in *Quetzalcoatl* she is left dubious by his proposal and decides to head back to Europe to think it over. This was where Lawrence's novel had reached by the middle of June 1923, and he evidently felt he had written enough for its completion to require very little more effort. He was enthusiastic about what he had already completed, as was Frieda, who referred to it as 'the most splendid thing he ever did'.[7] Lawrence felt he could now take a break and fell in with plans they had already made to travel back to the United States, where they could see Seltzer before taking the boat to Europe. He must have believed that he had written an answer to those who might say that, although he was quick to criticize other people's political schemes for the future (those of Ben Cooley, for example), he had none to offer of his own.

The Lawrences reached New Jersey towards the end of July 1923 and were able to stay in a cottage owned by the Seltzers (flatteringly named Birkindele). But then, with the prospect of catching the boat so imminent, Lawrence had one of his characteristic changes of mind and decided he did not want to return to Europe after all. Since Frieda was clearly not willing to accept his lord-and-mastership in this instance, it was decided they should separate and that she would rejoin him in America later (she sailed on 18 August). While they had been in America, there had been a reconciliation with Murry, which had perhaps begun with Lawrence's postcard to Mansfield from New Zealand and certainly continued after Lawrence wrote him a consolatory note on hearing that Mansfield had died in January 1923. Murry had recently taken over a journal called *The Adelphi* and, after having published slashing reviews of *The Lost Girl* and *Women in Love* elsewhere, had undergone a conversion, which resulted in his praising *Aaron's Rod* in *The Adelphi* ('much more important than *Ulysses*') and printing in that journal extracts from *Fantasia of the Unconscious*. Explaining why he felt he could not after all come back to England, Lawrence was now able to write to Murry: 'F. wants to see her children. And you know, wrong or not, I can't stomach the chasing of those Weekley children.' A week later, he explained that Frieda would probably arrive in Southampton on 26 or 27 September and added, 'I wish you would look after F. a bit.'[8] Similar requests he made to Catherine Carswell and S. S. Koteliansky do not have the same ironic ring as this one does in retrospect.

8
There and Back

The Lawrences appear to have held different views of their separation in August 1923. In all the letters he wrote shortly after Frieda left, Lawrence confidently assumed that his wife would rejoin him in North America, once she had seen her mother and children, but a letter Frieda sent to Adèle Seltzer from the boat by which she was travelling back to Southampton tells a different story. 'I am glad to be alone,' she wrote, 'and will not go back to him and his eternal hounding me, it's too ignominious! I will not stand his bad temper any more if I never see him again.'[1]

Once Frieda's ship had sailed, Lawrence headed back across the American continent for California, finally arriving in Los Angeles. There he was reunited with Knud Merrild and Kai Gøtzsche, whom he was hoping would accompany him back to Mexico – but Merrild was too busy, so it was only with Gøtzsche that, in late September, he set off down the Californian coast and headed for Lake Chapala. With the notion of establishing some kind of small community of like-minded friends never completely forgotten, he was on the lookout for a ranch he might buy, but the country he and Gøtzsche had to travel through was too rough even for his taste. Later, he would use his memories of it for the initial setting of his short story 'The Woman Who Rode Away', a grim tale of how a white woman who goes in search of a remote Native American tribe ends up as their human sacrifice.

Meanwhile, it was not like Lawrence to be without some other writing to preoccupy him. After Frieda's departure, he had received from Perth Mollie Skinner's attempt to write a novel set in the

Australian outback. How different this became, as he rewrote it, is difficult to judge given the absence of the original, but that he made one major change is evident from the precautions he took to warn Skinner about it, and from her shocked reaction when she was able to verify what it was. The hero of the novel is called Jack Grant and is attracted to two women. As, towards the end of the story, he sets off to found a little community of his own, far from civilization in the usual sense of that word, he sees no reason why he should not live together with both of them. One of the women refuses to fall in with this scheme, but there would be events that took place in Europe, once Lawrence was back there in the winter of 1923–4, which prompted him to imagine how she might be replaced with a willing substitute.

The notion of two women and one man (although not two men and one woman) cohabiting may have hovered in the back of Lawrence's mind because he was now on much better terms with Mabel Luhan, as Mabel Dodge was now called. No doubt aware that the Lawrences were separated, she had written to say that she now thought his analysis of her wilfulness correct and had declared herself ready to submit her judgement to his. He had responded encouragingly and at one point written that he would return to Taos soon and 'take [her] submission'.[2] This is a strange word to use, but it corresponds to a belief Lawrence held that women should always be subservient to men, however little practical effect his holding it may have had on his life with Frieda. In *The Ladybird*, that third novella he had written to accompany *The Fox* and *The Captain's Doll*, he had invented a Bohemian count who is a prisoner of war in England and has ideas about how society should be organized very like Lawrence's own (once men had freely chosen their own leaders, the count believes, they should never be allowed to question their judgements). Count Dionys is visited in an English hospital by Lady Daphne, a famous society beauty whom he had known before the war and who is equally aristocratic, although not very rich. Clearly based on Lady Cynthia Asquith, Lady Daphne is waiting for her husband to return at the end of the war. When he does so, both the psychological and physical wounds he has suffered make him unappealing, and she is far more strongly attracted to the diminutive, dark-haired Dionys, whom her husband has invited to stay with them in the two weeks before the Bohemian's expected repatriation. The situation which then develops anticipates *Lady Chatterley's Lover*, although with the husband freely agreeing to a cessation of his sexual relations with Lady Daphne while the count invites her to think of herself, in her nightly visits to him, only as his wife in the dark. The point here, however, is that in one of the husband's sexual encounters with his wife after his return from the war, he kisses her feet, whereas when she goes to visit the count in his bedroom, she embraces his.[3] As far as Lawrence was concerned, this last was the right way round.

By this stage in their marriage, the possibility of Frieda ever kissing Lawrence's feet was remote, and the letters he received indicated that she was having a good time. Having previously not got on very well with Murry, and still less well with Koteliansky (who had become the business manager of *The Adelphi*), she now spoke warmly of them both. Frieda confirmed the idea that, in the minds of these two, the journal's main purpose was to celebrate the genius of both Mansfield and Lawrence, and certainly a good deal of his work appeared in its pages. Perhaps remembering how savagely Murry had once reviewed *Women in Love*, Lawrence was not entirely convinced by his one-time friend's complete volte-face, but Frieda was insistent that he should come to London to see for himself and not at all inclined to join him in North America or Mexico. There was a battle of wills, which the accounts of Gøtzsche and others of how miserable Lawrence was without Frieda suggest he was always going to lose. Because Gøtzsche was also ready to go back to Europe, Lawrence offered to advance him his fare, and the two of them boarded a ship that would take them there from Veracruz. It sailed on 22 November 1923, not the best date for a man in Lawrence's state of health to be heading into a European winter.

Although he spent several of his first days in bed with his usual chest problems, Lawrence's experience of returning to London was much improved by both his reunion with Frieda and a warm welcome from old friends. Once he was on his feet again, and just before Christmas 1923, he decided to bring them all together in a celebratory dinner at the Café Royal. Apart from his wife and Murry, the party included the Carswells, Koteliansky, Mary Cannan and two painters Lawrence had known in the early war years, Mark Gertler and Dorothy Brett. Gertler had been responsible for a striking painting which had so impressed Lawrence that he had incorporated its subject of stiff, vacant-looking figures on a fairground roundabout into *Women in Love*. The paintings of Brett, as she was always known, seem to have been less familiar to him. Forty at the time of the dinner, she was hampered by deafness and had a capacity for devotion which had led her to spend a great deal of time caring for Mansfield in the last years of her life. After Mansfield's death, she had begun an affair with Murry that had been interrupted by the arrival of Frieda but resumed once Lawrence was back in London.

These last details are important for what happened at the Café Royal dinner, after more wine had been drunk than most of them – and Lawrence in particular – were used to. At some point, he stood up and made a heartfelt appeal for them all to join him in a community he would lead in North America, far removed from the evils of the modern world. 'I like you, Lawrence,' Mary Cannan is reported as replying, 'but not so much as all that, and I think you are asking what no human being has a right to ask of another.'[4] This is what most of the others ought to have replied, but instead, caught up in the occasion, they seem to have given Lawrence sufficient indications of complying to make him feel his appeal had been successful. Shortly afterwards, having been pressed to take some port, despite his insistence that it disagreed with him, he was sick on the table, became only partly conscious and had to be carried to a taxi so that he and Frieda could get back to their lodgings in Hampstead.

The only two guests who appeared to stand by their agreement to join Lawrence in America once the Café Royal dinner was over were Brett and Murry. In her case, with no domestic ties and a small private income, it could seem a reasonable decision (and she might at first have seen it as a way of continuing her affair with Murry); in his, it made little sense. He was not a writer who, like Lawrence, could function anywhere, but one who needed his contacts in the world of London journalism to earn his living. And yet throughout the Lawrences' remaining time in Europe there seems to have been an assumption that he would be of the party when they left. This makes even more strange the three short stories Lawrence had at least begun writing while he was still on European soil. One of these, 'Jimmy and the Desperate Women', is no more than a satire on Murry's sexual exploitation of *The Adelphi*'s female contributors, but in the other two, which are ghost/murder stories somewhat in the manner of Poe, an unmistakeable Murry figure meets a sticky end largely brought about by a version of Lawrence himself.

To understand why this should be so, one has to know that after Lawrence got back to London he began to suspect that Murry had been 'looking after' Frieda far more intimately than he had intended in his letter. Much later, Murry would record that although he and Frieda did fall in love in 1923, he had refrained from sleeping with her out of loyalty to her husband. Catherine Carswell was sceptical of his account, noting that because she occupied the flat below the one Frieda took when she first came to London, she was aware of how often Murry was up there. Whatever the truth, Lawrence must have felt that he had been cuckolded and took his revenge in the story he called 'The Border-Line'. In this, a character who has the recognizable physical characteristics of Murry but is called Philip Farquar meets his wife Katherine in Baden-Baden (whereas, in fact, Murry had accompanied Frieda for most of the train journey from London when she had been to see her mother there). Aware of how badly Philip compares with her former husband, Alan Anstruther, who died in the war, Katherine has begun to catch fleeting glimpses of the latter's ghost, and it is this ghost who later will make his way into the hotel where she and Philip are staying. By then lying on top of Philip, the ghostly Alan infects the man who has replaced him as Katherine's husband with what looks very like a terminal case of TB. After the now suffering husband has asked Katherine to comfort him by joining him in bed, Alan appears again and drags Philip out before subjecting his former wife to a strange form of intercourse in which he is like a pine tree penetrating her through all her pores, instead of the usual orifices, and yet nevertheless 'squeezing from her the last drop of her passion'.[5]

One of the many things that makes 'The Border-Line' so peculiar is the transparency of its compensatory mechanisms. It seems significant that it was written before Lawrence had been officially diagnosed with TB (a verdict he was to deny until the last weeks of his life), but the story also implies that, if Lawrence was no longer having normal sexual relations with Frieda, or not having them very often, whatever else he could offer was likely to be superior. Strangest of all, perhaps, is that all the complicated feelings that the story shows he felt towards Murry did not stop Lawrence accepting that he would soon be living in very close contact with him.

The third story adds to this puzzle, although its central female figure – the daughter of a peer, known only by her second name of James – is based not on Frieda but unequivocally on Brett (whose social background was similarly aristocratic). This character is deaf and carries with her a 'Marconi listening-machine', a battery-operated contrivance with headphones for amplifying sounds, one of which Brett did in fact own. In the story, James is described as 'having held herself intensely aloof from physical contact, and never let any man touch her', as seems to have been the case with Brett before her affair with Murry (which Lawrence was slow to learn about).

Leaving a house in Hampstead and saying goodbye to 'a thin man with a red beard' they call Lorenzo, James and her companion, Marchbanks – whose relatively small stature and bald patch Lawrence takes care to mention, as he had in his portrait of Murry in 'The Border-Line' – are caught in a snowstorm. As the snow is falling, James hears wild laughter and is able to glimpse its source among the nearby holly bushes. The idea that Lawrence then alludes to, rather than fully develops, is a collocation between his own return to Europe and that of Pan, the Greek god known for his propensity to laughter but also as the only being of his kind ever to have died. 'When Jesus was born,' Lawrence explained in a piece he was to dash off later for an American magazine in which his Santa Fe contact Willard Johnson was involved, 'the spirits wailed round the Mediterranean, Pan is dead. Great Pan is dead!'[6] Yet in the Hampstead of this story, 'He's come back. Aha! He's come back!' James hears several voices 'hallooing through the air'. It is the presence of Pan rather than the snowstorm that blows out the windows in the local church and sends its altar cloth flying (an abbreviated, semi-comic version of the way Ramón disposes of the Christian icons in the church at Chapala in *The Plumed Serpent*). The effect on James of having actually seen Pan is the recovery of her hearing, but, in the finale, the vision Marchbanks has of him has the quite different result often associated with humans seeing gods. With his white face 'distorted in a curious grin, that was chiefly agony, but partly wild recognition', Marchbanks pitches forward and dies on the carpet of James's studio, yelping, 'I knew it was he!'[7]

The world of Lawrence's imagination was very different from his experiences in life, but there seems no doubt he grew increasingly fond of Brett, as she did of him: in the final chapter of *The Boy in the Bush*, Jack Grant's disappointment at having one of the two women refuse to enter into a bigamous relationship is mitigated when a previously minor character called Hilda Blessington, who is now made to look and sound like Brett, agrees to take her place.[8] For the moment, however, after the Café Royal dinner, Lawrence left the one wife he certainly still had behind in London so that he could spend a few days around Christmas with his family, while Frieda may well have had more contact with her children, including her younger daughter, Barbara, who was still only nineteen but a rebellious art student at the Slade School of Fine Art (where both Brett and Gertler had trained) and not inclined to allow any supposed legal restrictions prevent her from being in touch with her mother. After briefly seeing his own relations, Lawrence spent a few days on the Welsh borders near Shrewsbury in order to meet Frederick Carter, an artist and writer who had previously sent him some work on the Book of Revelation he found interesting. Their discussions would bear fruit later, as would the setting in which they took place, since Lawrence would soon use it in one of his most celebrated novellas, *St. Mawr*. When he returned to London in late January

1924, it was to accompany Frieda on another visit to her mother in Baden-Baden. This may have seemed necessary now that it had been decided that she and Lawrence should return to New Mexico with however many of his Café Royal guests had finally agreed to come with them. In the event, when they left Southampton on 5 March, Brett was the only one with them, although Murry had given assurances that he would follow on later.

One of the reasons Lawrence was keen to get back to America was that he had heard disturbing rumours about Seltzer's business affairs, and, on landing in New York on 11 March 1924, he did indeed discover that they were in a parlous state. He was assured that the royalties he was owed would be paid eventually, but when, seven months later, he was to leave America, there was still a large sum owing to him. Having sensibly now decided to entrust his affairs to the U.S. branch of Curtis Brown, his literary agency in England, he and his two companions made their way to Taos and arrived on Mabel Luhan's estate on 22 March. She was temporarily absent, but when she returned a week or so later, full of her new spirit of submission, she was disappointed by the situation that faced her. Reconciled as she was to having to struggle with Frieda for Lawrence's attention, she now found there was another obstacle in the increasingly devoted Brett, who was becoming as attached to Lawrence as she had been to Mansfield. It may have been a special tribute to Mabel's generosity, therefore, that in April she gave all three an alternative place to live.[9] The first time the Lawrences were in Taos, she had dangled before them the prospect of a ranch of about 60 hectares (150 ac), located 3 kilometres (2 mi.) up the mountain from the cabins in which they would later stay with the Danes. She now decided to give this ranch not to Lawrence himself, since she had learnt the negative effects on him of feeling obliged, but to Frieda, who was otherwise without assets of any kind. The Lobo ranch, later renamed Kiowa by Lawrence after a Native American tribe of the area, was in a dilapidated state, which made it unpromising from a farming point of view, and had an estimated value of only about $1,200. It was a remarkable gift all the same, yet Lawrence could not rest easy until he had retrieved his manuscript of *Sons and Lovers* and given it to Mabel in recompense. As the market in manuscripts developed, Frieda was able to say that Mabel had enjoyed the better of the deal – but that was hardly the point.

Putting the ranch house, and a cabin where Brett could sleep, in order was a huge task into which Lawrence threw himself with great energy. He enjoyed being practical, as did Brett, whose aristocratic background meant that she had no problem with horses as the main means of transport. They had the help of a couple of local tradesmen but did a lot of homemaking themselves, although this did not mean that Lawrence neglected his writing. It was after he was able to settle into his new home that he wrote, or completed, his story about a bored white woman who 'rides away' in search of an obscure Native American tribe she has heard talk about, and whose members then mistake her for a victim it has been predicted their gods will send them, one whose sacrifice would end the domination of their own culture by Western values. Human sacrifice is a difficult phenomenon to contemplate, but in 'The Woman Who Rode Away' there is imaginative genius in the way Lawrence is able to envisage it from the tribe's point of view, however much that effort is bolstered by his own misogyny.

He named the long novella he was undoubtedly also writing at Kiowa after the stallion who plays such a prominent role in it: horses had always been a symbol of male potency for Lawrence, but, perhaps after having now learnt to ride one, never more so than in *St. Mawr*. Lou Carrington is a fashionable socialite who is immediately attracted to this horse and insists on buying it for her husband, Rico, to ride in Hyde Park despite the latter's nervousness and several indications that the animal might be difficult to manage. When the couple move down to the Shrewsbury area, which Lawrence had briefly seen on his visit to Carter, the social satire which comprises such a major part of *St. Mawr* shifts into top gear. Lou is an American from the South accompanied by her mother, the kind of middle-aged woman with a powerful personality of whom there are several in Lawrence's fiction after his encounter with Mabel Luhan. Called Mrs De Witt, she can be scathingly ironic about English society in

Dorothy Brett (1883–1977) in cowboy outfit.

its more effete or hidebound forms. Brett records Lawrence reading aloud to her and Frieda at Kiowa one scene in which this character scandalizes the local vicar and his wife and then comments, 'You laugh so much over it, that you have to stop. And we are laughing too.'[10] In recollections of Lawrence after his death, one of the most common accusations was that he had no sense of humour. This is obviously untrue, and there is abundant evidence that he could on occasions be playful and light-hearted. But there was also a vein in him of sardonic humour which tended to sound more bitter the older he grew. In Lou, who does not have her mother's wit, it reveals itself more as sardonic despair at the meaninglessness of the life she and her circle of well-heeled young friends are leading, and sometimes a dark and angry misanthropy that feels more like her creator's than her own.

Riding excursions in the Shrewsbury area allow both the character Lou and Lawrence himself to contrast the potency of St Mawr with the inadequate masculinity of young men like Rico. After his failure to control the horse results in injuries to both himself and one of his friends, the talk of having St Mawr gelded prompts Lou and her mother to take the horse away to America along with the only two people who know how to treat him, a Welsh groom called Lewis and Phoenix, a 'half-Indian' who has been with Mrs De Witt throughout. That her mother and Phoenix end up with Lou on a ranch in the Southwest offers Lawrence the opportunity of writing a reasonably detailed account of Kiowa, where the 'spirit of the place' is the opposite of what Lawrence unfairly imagines as Wordsworthian. This spirit of place is one to which Lou responds. Having contemplated but then rejected the idea of an affair with Phoenix, she tells her mother that there is something in the land that surrounds her 'more real to me than men are . . . It needs me. It craves for me. And to it, my sex is deep and sacred, deeper than I am, with a deep nature aware deep down of my sex.' After she has said that either having another relationship with a man will penetrate to her very soul or she will keep to herself, one is perhaps grateful that her mother is there to remark that, if that's the case, she may well have to keep to herself for a good while.[11]

By the time *St. Mawr* was being written, Murry was no longer expected. In May, he had written to give, as his reason for not keeping his promise to follow the others to America, the surprising news that he had only recently got married again (to one of *The Adelphi*'s young contributors). There was unlikely to have been much surprise in Kiowa at his non-appearance, or much distress in Brett at his marriage, given how close she now felt to Lawrence. Her attachment can hardly have pleased Frieda, although she may well have been glad of Brett's presence when, at the beginning of August, there was the first of what from then on would be a series of recurrent crises. No doubt confined to bed with one of his familiar chest complaints, Lawrence suddenly had a haemorrhage that caused bright-red blood to seep from his mouth. Having nursed Mansfield in her last years, Brett must have recognized at once what this colour usually meant. The local doctor was sent for and, without any tests, told Lawrence what he might well have made clear he wanted to hear: that the lungs were unaffected and the trouble came from his bronchial tubes. As he recovered, the patient was faced with what must have been a familiar dilemma for consumptives, who on the one hand were advised to avoid the cold while on the other they were told to seek out the clean, clear air of the mountains. With winter coming on, Lawrence decided (as he probably always intended) to head south, and in mid-October he set off with Frieda and Brett for Mexico City.

Lawrence's chief intention in going back to Mexico was to revise his Mexican novel, but it casts an interesting sidelight on the power of his visual memory that he felt no compulsion to do that in Chapala. He had always been interested in Oaxaca as a possible future destination, and in Mexico City he met at the British consulate a man called Constantine Rickards, whose brother happened to be a priest there. It was to Oaxaca, therefore, that the trio moved in the second week of November, Brett settling herself in a hotel while the Lawrences rented a part of Father Edward Rickards's large house where Lawrence could begin turning *Quetzalcoatl* into *The Plumed Serpent*. Although the finished novel turned out almost twice as long as the first version, the only major change was that Kate, now

The Lawrences in Oaxaca, Mexico, in 1924.

surnamed Leslie rather than Burns, marries Cipriano, in whom she recognizes 'the ancient phallic mystery, the ancient god-devil of the male Pan'. 'When the power of his blood rose in him, the dark aura streamed from him like a cloud pregnant with power,' Lawrence writes, and this produces in Kate 'a mystery of prone submission . . . Submission absolute'. The effect of his lovemaking is to suppress in her 'the seething, frictional seething Aphrodite', which she now realizes she never really wanted, and replace it with a 'new, soft, heavy, hot flow, when she was like a fountain gushing noiseless'.[12]

The other changes to *Quezalcoatl* are superficial, relating mainly to how Ramón and Cipriano's new religion operates from a ceremonial point of view. Always interested in clothes, Lawrence added numerous details about the costumes that are worn and wrote a whole series of hymns which could be sung or intoned. One consequence of these amplifications is to make it seem that what the two men have created is indeed a cult rather than a religion, especially as there is very little new information about dogma, or the social and political implications of the new movement. He did introduce a number of impressive local improvements which could help to explain why E. M. Forster could consider *The Plumed Serpent* the best of Lawrence's novels.[13] In spite of these, for many readers the general result of the extra material is to make the work heavier and harder to get through. While he was in Oaxaca, Lawrence wrote four charming sketches about his life there. Put together with three essays about ceremonial Indian dances he had written in Taos, these would later be published under the title *Mornings in Mexico*. There is a case for suggesting that this book says more for his value as a writer than *The Plumed Serpent*, although it is one he himself would have certainly disputed.

To the strain of revising *Quetzalcoatl* was added a domestic difficulty. Because she did his typing, Brett was a great help to Lawrence and increasingly came to appreciate what she would later call, in a memoir, 'the real aristocracy of [his] heart and mind'.[14] Frieda also thought her husband was a special kind of person, but that did not make it any less irritating to have an adoring Brett always at Lawrence's shoulder, and she eventually decided she could take no more. She accused Brett of being like a spinster who falls in love with the local vicar, implying that her relationship was worse for being sexless – although, if there had been a ménage à trois in the usual sense, Frieda was hardly likely to have been more accepting. She told Lawrence that Brett had to go and put him in the difficult position of worrying how safely a woman of her age, in a Mexico still not free of revolutionary upheavals, could make her way back to Taos on her own, although that is what Frieda now insisted Brett did.

Frieda's implied sneer at Brett's lack of sexual experience could have been a faint echo of a novella her husband had written back in Kiowa, called *The Princess*. This concerns a woman with a sheltered background who, partly because of a diminutive physique, has remained a virgin into early middle age. She takes a trip into the wilder part of New Mexico with a Mexican guide who has been reduced to this status even though, in his own culture, his background is as privileged as hers – someone who is (as it were) a dispossessed prince. When circumstances lead to their passing the night together in the same hut, the cold leads the woman to encourage the guide to warm her up. What follows satisfies her curiosity but also shows her how alien sexual activity is to her nature. She refuses any further intimacy with the guide, but this so offends his male pride that he throws her clothes in a nearby lake and keeps her as his sexual captive until the authorities appear and shoot him. While his death leaves the woman apparently unmoved, the narrative clearly suggests it is at least partly her fault. Lawrence thought at one point that this novella might go well with 'The Woman Who Rode Away' and *St. Mawr*, making up a volume similar to the one that had contained *The Fox*, *The Ladybird* and *The Captain's Doll*. Certainly, *The Princess* is as well written as the other two novellas with New Mexican settings and has a tighter, more satisfying structure than *St. Mawr*, although, as he recognized, it could hardly lift the gloom the others might be inclined to encourage. Any relation of the novella to Brett is distant, and even if she perceived it she was too devoted to Lawrence to have protested.

The distress he experienced in having to tell Brett to leave is unlikely to have any connection with the fact that, three weeks after her departure on 19 January 1925, he fell seriously ill. His symptoms were similar to those he had suffered in Sri Lanka, with fever and severe intestinal pains, so that he later attributed them to malaria, although he then added 'and a typhoid condition inside, and flu making my chest go wrong'.[15] Whatever the illness was, it was grave enough to have Frieda move him on a stretcher to a hotel and then decide to seek expert medical attention at the American hospital in Mexico City. By the time he saw the doctors there, the crisis point appears to have passed, but after examining him one of them, in his presence and that of his wife, announced dryly, 'Mr Lawrence has tuberculosis.'[16] Their plan had been to sail back to Europe from Veracruz, but the doctors strongly advised against this and said that mountain air would be the best way of prolonging his life. Getting out of Mexico and into the United States was not easy because of new legislation aimed at restricting entry to those suffering from TB, but with the help of a little rouge to disguise Lawrence's greenish pallor they were able to cross the border and arrive back at their Kiowa ranch at the beginning of April.

Waiting to greet them was, of course, Brett. Frieda quickly tried to establish protocols, one of which included Brett having to blow a whistle on approaching Kiowa so that she could be sent

Kiowa Ranch, Taos, where the Lawrences lived.

back to the accommodation she had found nearby were her visit not convenient. It is doubtful these were effective or lasted long, especially as, with Lawrence quickly returning to activity, there was so much to do on the ranch. By cleaning out a spring 3 kilometres (2 mi.) away, he had previously managed to establish a meagre water supply, and now he not only planted an alfalfa field but acquired some hens and even a cow, from the milk of which Frieda made butter. The resulting activities prompted fresh thought about the kind of relationships one ought to have with the natural world, which Lawrence expressed in several essays, including one entitled 'Reflections on the Death of a Porcupine'. Porcupines were pests in the area surrounding Kiowa, and when he had first driven Lawrence up there, Tony Luhan had shot one. This had made him angry, but now he encountered the necessity of having to shoot one himself, although at the same time he was insistent, in his essay, on the need to establish proper relationships with those other animals one did not have to shoot, including his hens and his cow, one that avoided what he called 'anthropomorphic lust'.[17] When his reflections on the porcupine were published, it was in a volume with that same title, together with six lightly revised essays originally intended for *The Signature*, the last three of which had never been in print before because his and Murry's journal had collapsed before they had time to appear.

Lawrence was happy trying his hand at farming, but he kept on writing – and not only essays. Prompted by a member of Mabel's circle called Ida Rauh, who had been an actress, to try his hand again at drama, he wrote a play called *David*, which is largely an adaption of the Bible's account of that figure's conflicts with Saul. But there seems to have been an agreement with Frieda that they would return to Europe in the autumn, and the visa on which he had been able to enter the United States was in any case only valid for six months. In early September, therefore, he prepared to leave Kiowa, suspending the furniture from the ceilings to avoid the pack rats and suggesting to Brett that, although she should not travel with him, they might meet up later in Capri, where he had heard his friends the Brewsters were once again established. Seltzer's financial troubles had obliged

Lawrence to move to a much bigger, more secure publishing firm (Knopf), and they meant that, after purchase of the boat tickets, he had very little in the bank, although that was nothing new. On 21 September 1925, he left New York, the American excursus, although he may not have believed or known it, now finally over.

9
Lady Chatterley's Lover

Before leaving America, Lawrence was assured by Seltzer that he would do his best to pay him the outstanding royalties, bit by bit. When he arrived in London, he must have been relieved that at least the person who had now become his main English publisher, Martin Secker, was solvent. He had an Italian wife who came from Spotorno, a town on the Italian Riviera, and she told the Lawrences about a house there, the top storeys of which were for rent. It was owned by the wife of a 35-year-old officer in the Bersaglieri regiment, Angelo Ravagli, and, having moved on to Italy and inspected the apartments, the Lawrences decided to rent them. As winter advanced, the heating systems in the Villa Bernarda would prove less than ideal, but Lawrence was happy there. With views of the sea and the pleased feelings that came from being back in Italy, he would declare that he now had no wish to return to New Mexico, although this thought may have been prompted by a suspicion, which he did not articulate, that the new health regulations meant that he never could.

One of the first visitors to the Villa Bernarda was Frieda's younger daughter, Barbara, always known by friends and family as Barby. Lawrence became warmly attached to Barby, and she gave him many details of her upbringing after Frieda had left Ernest Weekley and he took his children to a house in a London suburb, where his elderly parents and an unmarried sister could help him look after them. It was from these accounts that he constructed one of the best of his novellas, or indeed of all his fiction, *The Virgin and the Gipsy*. The Barby figure is there called Yvette, with the head of her family a Reverend Mr Saywell, who is clearly based on Ernest Weekley. He has been deserted by his wife and lives with an unmarried sister full of rancorous envy of the youthful, heedless Yvette and his old mother, who still exerts psychological control over her son – and who is memorably characterized by Lawrence as like an old toad sitting outside a beehive, snapping up the bees as they launch out, 'as if it could consume the whole hive-full, into its aging, bulging, purse-like wrinkledness'.[1] The staleness and stifling moral conformity of this household are memorably evoked, so much so that again one might think of Austen, although an Austen in a particularly bilious and misanthropic mood.

Yvette finds the various young men she dates unsatisfactory but is attracted by a local Gipsy, who is already married and happens to be in the area. Like so many other of Lawrence's male figures who are outside the usual social orbit of his female protagonists, he has a sexual allure that fascinates her. In the finale, there is a flood which sweeps away the rectory where the Saywells live, and while the old matriarch is drowned, Yvette is rescued from the same fate by the arrival of the Gipsy, who protects her from hypothermia by taking off her sodden clothes and pressing his warm, naked body against hers. That they do not necessarily have sex is part of the success of the novella, which shifts effectively between social realism and a fairy tale in which the heroine is the sleeping princess. It is surprising that, aware as he must have been of his story's value, Lawrence decided against publication once it was completed. The only clue we have to his reasons for this decision is Barby's later report that Frieda had shown her the manuscript and given as her late husband's reasons for holding it back that 'after all, he is their father', the 'he' being of course Weekley.[2]

Lawrence must have begun to regret the inadequate heating in the Villa Bernarda when, after Christmas, it turned very cold. In February 1926, he reported to Brett that he had had another 'bronchial haemorrhage like at the ranch'.[3] This happened to be a time when, in addition to Frieda's two daughters, his sister Ada was visiting the Lawrences with a friend. Many of the tensions which then developed could probably be traced back to the conviction

Ada had developed in 1919 that Frieda did not know how to look after her brother properly. The strained atmosphere meant that when Ada was ready to go home, and Lawrence was more or less recovered, he decided to accompany her at least as far as Nice, where she and her friend were due to take a boat. In what was virtually another marital separation, he then made his way to Capri in order to see the Brewsters, but also Brett, who had meanwhile returned to Europe and, following his advice, landed up there.
At some point, when Lawrence and Brett were in nearby Amalfi, he made two attempts to have sex with her, both of which were miserable failures ('Your pubes are all wrong,' she very much later reported him as saying).[4] An unhappy Brett then began the long journey back to Kiowa, while Lawrence, having found in Frieda's recent communications a more conciliatory note, returned to Spotorno. If before his absence Frieda had not already begun her affair with her landlady's husband, Angelo Ravagli, it was almost certainly established while he was away and was to continue, when circumstances permitted, for the rest of Lawrence's life, as well as long after.

With the lease on the Villa Bernarda about to expire, the Lawrences decided to visit Florence in April and found, outside the city, another top storey available in what was called (after its owner) the Villa Mirenda. Since the annual rent for these spacious rooms came to only £25, they were able to use them as a pied-à-terre for the next two years. Set on a hill in the middle of beautiful Tuscan countryside, the villa had three peasant families associated with it. Lawrence would get to know them quite well, and of course he still had friends in Florence itself who were not very far away.

One of these with whom he did not immediately re-establish contact was Norman Douglas, largely because of a pamphlet Douglas had published in 1925 called *A Plea for Better Manners*. This began by noting that, although Lawrence had stipulated that 50 per cent of the royalties from the sale of Magnus's *Memoirs of the Foreign Legion* should go to the Maltese from whom its author had borrowed money before his suicide, he had kept the other half for himself, despite documents which made it quite plain that

The Brewsters in Capri with their daughter, Dorothy Brett and D. H. Lawrence, 1926.

Magnus had wanted Douglas to be his literary executor. Lawrence had responded by suggesting that it was only because of the long introduction he had provided that the memoir had appeared but also that, in a letter sent to him in December 1921, Douglas had explicitly said, 'By all means do what you like with the MS' and 'Pocket all the cash yourself,' adding that the Maltese was too much of a fool to deserve any. Because Lawrence still had a copy of this letter, he had been able to take the wind out of Douglas's sails, on this somewhat tricky issue at least.

The other main charge in *A Plea for Better Manners* was more difficult to refute. In a lively and engaging manner, Douglas appeared to pass over the way he himself had been depicted, not only in Lawrence's introduction but previously in *Aaron's Rod*, yet went on to claim that this habit of writers basing their characters on people they knew was not only ungentlemanly but misleading. The portrait Lawrence had drawn of Magnus, Douglas claimed, made him seem much less agreeable and serious-minded than he had in fact been and was the result of a method that involved selecting for literary purposes 'two or three facets of a man or woman' and disregarding all the others in a way that 'falsifies life'.[5]

Douglas was making what was in the end a quite genial public protest about his appearances in Lawrence's books, but there had always been others who expressed their resentment differently. In 1926, Lawrence would write a story called 'The Man Who Loved Islands'. Because Compton Mackenzie was well known for having recently bought several islands, he put pressure on Secker, who happened to be his publisher as well as Lawrence's, not to have this story republished in a collection, even though it is clearly more about its author's own struggles with the impulse to isolate oneself from other human beings than about Mackenzie's. It seems likely that he was prompted into this action less by 'The Man Who Loved Islands' than by another story that Lawrence had written a little earlier, called 'Two Blue Birds'. This is full of details that Faith Mackenzie had told Lawrence in confidence about the state of her marriage to Compton and which she never expected him to use. She was in a long line of women who had reason to feel that they had

Lawrence at Villa Mirenda, near Florence.

been betrayed, beginning with Jessie Chambers and Helen Corke, including the intermediate cases of Lady Ottoline and Mabel Luhan, and even encompassing Lady Cynthia Asquith, to whom Lawrence always remained strongly attracted.

Lawrence had warned Lady Cynthia at the time that a short story he had written during the war called 'The Thimble' contained

her portrait, and identifiable references to her and her family
were increased in number when they were used as the basis for
The Ladybird, the novella in which the Lady Cynthia figure stops
having sexual relations with her war-wounded husband in order
to initiate an affair with the dark and mysterious Count Dionys.
Following the war, Lady Cynthia had experienced some financial
difficulties and, after taking a job as J. M. Barrie's secretary, had
begun to edit books. One of these was a collection of stories of
the supernatural, to which she asked Lawrence to contribute. His
first attempt was written around Christmas 1925 to early 1926 and
called 'Glad Ghosts'. She felt that, apart from its sexual content,
this story was too long and likely to be unpublishable, before then
adding that it contained 'another portrait of me which makes it
more difficult'.[6] Perhaps because he was fond of Lady Cynthia,
Lawrence tried again and produced almost immediately a story so
striking that it was included not only in her anthology, but in very
many others afterwards. It was called 'The Rocking Horse Winner'
and gave Asquith a great deal of distress. This was not because she
was particularly recognizable as the mother of the little boy who
rides himself to death on his rocking horse – although only after his
rocking allows him to predict the winners of horse races and thereby
provide her with the money he instinctively realizes she craves. It
was rather that, as Lawrence well knew, the Asquiths had an autistic
child to whom, the story might imply, their own struggles to solve
their financial difficulties had led them to pay insufficient attention.
It was as if, Lady Cynthia appears to have felt, in writing the story
Lawrence had found a way of blaming her for her child's autism.

    The Lawrences had no sooner begun to settle into the Villa
Mirenda than they were off again on their travels: Frieda to
Baden-Baden on a promised visit to her mother, and Lawrence
more directly back to England because there was expected to be a
production of his play *David* there, and he wanted to be on hand
to see it. Two friendships he renewed when he arrived in London –
with Richard Aldington and Aldous Huxley – would be important
for his remaining years of life. With the expected production
hanging fire, he went north in August to join Ada and other

Aldous Huxley, September 1931, bromide print.

members of his family on holiday in Mablethorpe and afterwards spent some time with them in their homes. This would be his last visit to his native regions and was to provide him with many fresh details for the setting of *Lady Chatterley's Lover*. It would remind him of the beauty of the countryside, which he renders so memorably in that novel, but also make him aware of new buildings in and around the pits that would have confirmed his horror of the kind of encroaching industrialization of which, in its final version, he makes Clifford Chatterley a keen proponent. After travelling from Germany to England and spending some time with her children in London, Frieda was with her husband in the Midlands by late August, but in September they moved back to Hampstead before returning to Italy at the end of that month.

Installed once again in the Villa Mirenda, the Lawrences were visited by Aldington and also Huxley, who came in a car accompanied by his wife, Maria. She had a brother who was a painter and brought with her several spare canvases to give to Lawrence, a gift which was to launch him on a whole new alternative career. In his youth, he had been a reasonably gifted amateur, and from time to time since then had painted what were mostly copies of famous pictures; now he began to produce large canvases of his own. It was a welcome relaxation from what had been, and continued to be, the life of almost continual writing by which he earned his living, an escape into another world – except that, with a brush rather than a pen in hand, he continued his fight against that privileging of the mind over the body which he believed to be such a disabling feature of Western culture. Nearly all the many human figures in the pictures he painted, usually in scenes of love or dancing, would be nudes.

It was now that Lawrence embarked on what would be the first version of *Lady Chatterley's Lover*. There were difficulties in the initial conception of this novel that help to explain how he came to write it three times. As nearly all the world now knows, the story concerns a young woman whose aristocratic husband has returned from the war paralysed in the lower half of his body and who finds alternative physical satisfaction with a man from the lower classes, her husband's gamekeeper. What her relations would be with this man after or between their sexual encounters, given their very different educational and cultural backgrounds, is an issue which would not arise were he quasi-symbolic, like an equivalent figure is in *The Virgin and the Gipsy* – but Lawrence was not always inclined to deal with matters in this way, or indeed to brush them aside. As far back as 'The Daughters of the Vicar', he had tried to imagine how a vicar's daughter would fare in a marriage with a miner, and at the end of *The Lost Girl* he had offered a bleak vision of his educated heroine's future as the wife of an Italian with a peasant background. In the first version of *Lady Chatterley's Lover*, the character who will eventually be named Mellors is called Parkin. After the scandal of his affair with Constance Chatterley has forced him to give up gamekeeping, he takes a job in a steelworks in Sheffield, where he lodges with a work colleague and his family. In an excellent scene in which Parkin invites Connie to tea with this family, the problems that social differences can make are very effectively raised, and the reader is made painfully aware of the illusion that love and sex can conquer all, all of the time. It was as if Lawrence had always ringing in his ears what we can legitimately imagine as a real-life exchange with his mother which he incorporated into *Sons and Lovers*: from the middle classes, Paul Morel says, 'one gets ideas, and from the common people – life itself, warmth.' 'It's all very well, my boy,' his mother replies, 'but then why don't you go and talk to your father's pals?'[7] In this first version of his last novel, Parkin is made defiantly working class throughout and turns out to be the secretary of the communist league in the steelworks. Socially, culturally and even politically ill-matched as he and Connie are, there are no detailed descriptions of their lovemaking to help explain what keeps them together.

A second difficulty is that Clifford Chatterley's sexual inadequacy is not just that which, in his later writings, Lawrence was inclined to attribute to all young men in the generation just below him (especially if they were middle class). Rather, it has been brought about by the war and was therefore bound to excite sympathy in many of his potential readers. There is not much evidence that Lawrence shared that sympathy. How limited it could be is clear from his treatment of Lady Daphne's husband in *The Ladybird*, but also relevant here are passages in Section Five of 'The Crown', which had never been published before Lawrence included them in his *Reflections on the Death of a Porcupine* collection. These relate to a disabled soldier he had seen on the seafront at Bognor in 1915:

> The maimed soldier, strong and handsome, with some of the frail candour of the newly awakened child in his face, came slowly down the pier on his crutches ... the people stared at him with a sort of fascination. So he was rather vain, rather proud, like a vain child ... He was rather vain and slightly ostentatious, not as a man with a wound, a trophy, more as a child who is conspicuous among envious elders ... The women particularly were fascinated.[8]

For Lawrence, any serious damage to the body was always going to mean damage to the psyche, and from the start he presents Clifford as having a certain cold egotism, the egotism of the maimed survivor. Throughout the three versions, he worked to justify Connie's treatment of him by making Clifford increasingly unpleasant, yet could never quite shake off the idea that his impotence is not exactly his fault, and in Lawrence's later defence of this novel, which he called *A Propos of Lady Chatterley's Lover*, he was to write:

> When I read the first version, I recognised that the lameness of Clifford was symbolic of the paralysis, the deeper emotional or passional paralysis, of most men of his sort and class, today. I realised it was perhaps taking an unfair advantage of Connie, to paralyse him technically. It made it so much more vulgar of her to leave him. Yet the story came as it did, by itself, so I left it alone.[9]

Having finished his first version of his novel at a daily rate of over 2,000 words, Lawrence began almost immediately to write the second. In *John Thomas and Lady Jane*, as this second version of *Lady Chatterley* became known, he filled out what had previously been sketchy, with more details of the local setting, for example, and with the introduction or further development of minor characters such as Connie's father and Mrs Bolton, the nurse who is hired to look after Clifford (a brilliant conception). The novel is now less political and Parkin no longer a communist: 'I was so afraid you were just going to deteriorate into a socialist or a fascist, or something dreary and political,' Connie tells him. But this does not mean that the class antagonism which Lawrence felt he had detected on his recent visit to England is any less pervasive. Making Clifford, with his 'survivor complex' and 'terrible passion for self-preservation', more unpleasant helps to explain why the miners should now hate him so much. In the first version, he had enjoyed an intellectual companionship with Connie, so much so that she had initially thought she needed both her husband and her lover, the one for the mind and the other for the body. In the second version, nearly all traces of that accommodation have disappeared, and there is a new emphasis on the importance of 'touch' and on the extraordinary transformative power of sexual intercourse. Frieda claimed that *Lady Chatterley* was the 'romantic novel' Lawrence had always talked of wanting to publish, and *John Thomas and Lady Jane* was well on the way to that, except that now, with love scenes that were so much more explicit, it was also well on the way to being unpublishable.[10]

With the ending of *John Thomas and Lady Jane* still indeterminate, Lawrence broke off writing in March 1927 in order to collect Earl Brewster and embark with him on a tour of Etruscan sites which they had been planning for some time. Meanwhile, Frieda made another visit to her mother (and perhaps Ravagli). How much Lawrence enjoyed the Etruscan trip is apparent in the tone of the account he wrote of it, once he was back in Florence. He and Brewster visited four of the well-known Etruscan centres – Cerveteri, Tarquinia, Vulci and Volterra – and Lawrence was delighted with what he saw in all of them. But it was in the painted tombs of Tarquinia that he felt he had at last come across a culture that offered a viable alternative to the modern world. As far as the Etruscans were concerned, he conjectured (very little was known about them), life was as joyful after death as before. Their delightful painted figures of men striding along in their tunics and playing on their pipes suggested a people in perfect harmony with their environment and exhibited a sense of proportion that he saw as a consequence of what he now called 'phallic consciousness' (Brewster had pointed out to him that there were phallic symbols at the entry

Etruscan fresco, Tomb of the Lionesses, Tarquinia, Italy, 6th century BC.

to most of the tombs). 'And so they move on,' he writes of one of these pipe players, 'on their long sandalled feet, pass the little berried olive-trees, swiftly going with their limbs full of life, full of life to the tips.'[11] What the paintings indicated was a way of living with nature and other people that was in direct contrast with that of the Romans, who were assumed to have wiped the Etruscans out, and whom Lawrence associated with the contemporary fascist regime in Italy, only concerned with brutal power and money-making. The painted banqueting scenes in the tombs showed that, unlike the Romans in Lawrence's understanding of them, men and women ate together, and he was particularly taken with one painting that shows a couple at a meal together, with the man leaning forward to touch the woman under the chin with a 'delicate caress'. 'Here,' he comments, 'in this faded Etruscan painting, there is a quiet flow of touch that unites the man and woman on the couch, the timid boy behind, the dog that lifts its nose, even the very garlands than hang from the wall.'[12] This is the new emphasis that had become so important for *Lady Chatterley's Lover*. There is plenty of biographical evidence that Lawrence himself nearly always disliked being touched, which was one of the reasons why the medical examinations during the war were so traumatic for him, and he often referred to the 'noli me tangere' of the resurrected

Christ, but there was a kind of touch of which he approved, and it was one he felt the Etruscans knew all about.

Either before or after his Etruscan tour, Lawrence responded to yet another request from Lady Cynthia, this time for a murder story. In some ways, he was the right person to approach, given that his attitude to violence and physical assault was a long way from being conventionally humanitarian. What had complicated his stance during the war was that he was in no way a pacifist. He accepted fully that there were homicidal impulses in himself, as there were in the orderly in 'The Prussian Officer', and since he believed that morality consisted in fulfilling one's deepest urges, he could hardly subscribe wholeheartedly to the sixth commandment. This is why, in *Women in Love*, Birkin does not blame Hermione Roddice for trying, in effect, to kill him, although he of course recognizes that individuals have an equal right to do all they can to avoid being killed, not to be what he describes as one of those 'murderees' without which the killing cannot take place (a murderee is essentially what the character Banford becomes when the young man in Lawrence's rewritten version of *The Fox* makes sure that the tree he is cutting down should fall on her). Struggling with the natural environment in New Mexico had strengthened Lawrence's conviction that there was no use pretending that all was sweetness and light. 'The Apache warrior in his war paint,' he claimed in one of the essays he wrote there, which describes Native American dancing and is called 'Indians and Entertainment', 'shrieking the war cry and cutting the throats of old women, still he is part of the mystery of creation. He is godly as the growing corn.'[13]

For a man with these views, the 'murder' Lawrence came up with in the story he wrote for Lady Cynthia will seem a disappointingly mild affair. The victim in 'The Lovely Lady' is a once-beautiful old woman, whose death is engineered by her niece when she uses a drainpipe as a speaking tube so that she can give the impression of a voice from beyond the grave. Anxious to overcome maternal opposition to her own marriage with the old lady's remaining son, the niece speaks on behalf of the vengeful spirit of an elder boy who had died after his relations with a young woman had been ruined by his mother. The voice so shocks the old lady, and so excites her residual guilt, that she suffers a complete and grotesque physical meltdown of the kind Poe describes in 'Ligeia', and dies. The interest here is not so much in whether bringing about someone else's death in this way should be classed as murder, but rather in reading another protest, after *The Virgin and the Gipsy*, against the stifling of the young by the old. It is tempting to recall how, in the summary of *Sons and Lovers* Lawrence wrote for Garnett, it is strongly implied that Mrs Morel is responsible for the death of Paul's elder brother. Lawrence's recent, final visit to Eastwood would lead to a series of short autobiographical pieces in which he describes his own family relationships. Often in these what had been the commanding narrative structure of *Sons and Lovers*, in which the mother is the long-suffering heroine, is reversed, and his mother blamed for her middle-class efforts to see that her children 'got on'.

In July 1927, Lawrence fell as ill as he had been in Oaxaca. But this time his troubles had begun with a major haemorrhage, making the reason for them plain enough. Anxious doctors recommended that he escape the summer heat of Florence, and the Lawrences had already been thinking about visiting Frieda's younger sister, Johanna, in a lakeside resort near to Villach in Austria – but, since Lawrence was too weak to walk, they had some difficulty in getting him there. Once he did arrive, and after a move to the holiday home of Frieda's other sister, in southern Bavaria, he slowly improved, although from this time on he would rarely be free of a persistent cough, and his failure to regain the weight he had lost during his illness was a constant worry. Making his way back to Italy with Frieda, he stopped in Baden-Baden and was persuaded to try an 'inhalation cure' on offer there, the original feature of which was a steam supposedly impregnated with radium. Having often taken, in New Mexico, a patent medicine for chest complaints called Solution Patanberge, he now brought back from Germany a 'Brust-thee' and later he would be persuaded by his English relatives to try a medicine called Umckaloabo from the Consumption Cure Company. Not that Lawrence accepted that he was consumptive: until almost the end but he kept insisting that the problem was not in his lungs but in his bronchial tubes. While he was in his sister-in-law's Bavarian house, she had arranged a visit from a Munich writer she knew who happened also to be a doctor. He seems to have confirmed Lawrence in his belief that his problems stemmed from the bronchi, but a little later confided to a colleague, 'An average man with those lungs would have died long ago.'[14]

Being ill, and temporarily out of commission, increased Lawrence's worries about his income, especially as doctors and inhalation cures were expensive. But back in Italy, at the Villa Mirenda, he was fit enough to set to work on *Collected Poems*, which Secker had long ago suggested to him. Going over all the poems he had written in the past must have revived some painful memories, but for someone who held fast to a romantic aesthetic of spontaneity, the process also posed a theoretical problem: how far was he entitled to correct and hopefully improve words which must have seemed to his younger self the right ones? The solution he adopted was to explain in an introduction that, in his earlier days, the 'demon' that inspired his work often had its hand over its mouth, and his alterations and corrections were therefore what he had wanted and should have said at the time, had he not been inhibited. A particularly flagrant example of the difference Lawrence's revisions made is a poem called 'Virgin Youth', which had appeared in the collection *Amores* in 1916. In many ways, this startling piece illustrates how Lawrence had always been a controversial writer in that it describes the way in which a period of sexual frustration eventuates in either masturbation or spontaneous emission, a 'bursten flood'. But the terms are vague, and the episode implied rather than made explicit. For *Collected Poems*, Lawrence more than doubled the length of the original poem and added entirely new material, including this address to an erect penis:

> Dark, ruddy pillar, forgive me! I
> Am helplessly bound
> To the rock of virginity. Thy
> Strange voice has no sound.
> We cry in the wilderness. Forgive me, I

Would so gladly lie
In the womanly valley, and ply
Thy twofold dance.

Thou dark one, thou proud, curved beauty! I
Would worship thee, letting my buttocks prance.
But the hosts of men with one voice deny
Me the chance.[15]

This is less the young man whose demon had a hand over its mouth than the writer who, in embarking on the third and final version of *Lady Chatterley's Lover*, had decided to put behind him his long history of troubles with censorship and write exactly what he felt like writing.

It is doubtful whether Lawrence would have made this decision had he not been reconciled to Douglas. The two had met in the Florence bookshop of Douglas's close friend, Pino Orioli, several months before and decided to bury the hatchet. At this time, Douglas was making a modest income by publishing, via Orioli, a series of short books on a subscription basis for what would now be described as a niche market: short studies on often arcane scholarly matters. Different though his latest novel was from these, it must have struck Lawrence that he could avoid the problems of censorship *Lady Chatterley's Lover* was certain to encounter by publishing in the same way. Remembering how notoriety had boosted the sales of *Women in Love*, he may also have calculated that, in this way, he could make some money, or at least be sure of breaking even (private publication having the obvious disadvantage of an initial investment of capital). *John Thomas and Lady Jane* already contained words like 'cunt' and 'fuck' and some sexual details, but once he abandoned the idea of sending the work to Secker or Knopf, he could be increasingly uninhibited in describing the lovemaking between Connie and the gamekeeper, now renamed Mellors. His descriptions of orgasm had necessarily to remain metaphorical, and in his account of the 'night of sensual passion' that Connie and Mellors experience before she leaves for Venice, anal intercourse is only suggested rather than made explicit, but in the other lovemaking scenes, he was now much more specific in describing their sexual encounters, referring directly to parts of their bodies in ways in which publication in the usual fashion would have made impossible.

Other changes Lawrence made to *Lady Chatterley* were associated with another meeting in Florence, but one which took place after he had been ill. In November 1927 he ran into Dikran Kouyoumdjian, the friend of Philip Heseltine who had stayed with the Lawrences for a few weeks during the war years in Cornwall. Now the rich and successful author of an international bestseller called *The Green Hat* (he told Lawrence that an American dramatization of this work had earned him more than $5,000 in a single week), Michael Arlen, as Kouyoumdjian was now known, was almost immediately incorporated into Lawrence's rewriting as Michaelis, an Irish dramatist who has been unusually successful in attracting the attention of what in the final version of the novel is referred to persistently as 'the bitch goddess of success', and who precedes Mellors as Connie's lover. Even though the aristocratic Clifford despises Michaelis as someone whose new-found wealth cannot disguise his standing as a social upstart, he invites him to his country house because he himself is now a writer of short stories desperate for both critical and commercial success. The way Michaelis is regarded by Clifford, and by the group of his friends who discuss sex in a flippant, avant-garde fashion, excites Connie's sympathy, even if as a lover he also demonstrates the sexual inadequacy of the rising generation. Ejaculating too soon, Michaelis is nonetheless able to keep his erect penis inside her while she achieves her own climax, 'grinding her own coffee', as Mellors will later say in reference to the sexual habits of the wife from whom he is separated, Bertha Coutts.[16]

Another change Lawrence made to his novel, more significant than his introduction of Michaelis, is in his treatment of Mellors. Much closer now than before to his creator, with both a weak chest and a sexual history that sounds very like Lawrence's own, he has been an officer during the war and is sufficiently well educated to more than hold his own with people like Clifford, switching to dialect only in moments of tenderness with Connie, or when he wants to be deliberately offensive. Desperate about the way industrialization has laid waste to the countryside and the search for money has separated people from natural instinctive contact with both each other and their surroundings, he can now see no political solution to the disaster he observes around him. His temporary answer has been the wood over which he has some charge, and in which he has sex with Connie. Lawrence wondered whether Clifford's wound was symbolic. Since he is now represented as not only an aspiring author but, like Gerald in *Women in Love*, a modernizing mine owner, what certainly qualifies as symbolic is an effective scene in which his motorized bath chair careers through the wood, crushing all the flowers in its way. Since the upper and middle classes are so corrupt – a passage in which Mellors denounces the latter is quite spectacularly vitriolic – and since, with their searching after money and mindless entertainment, the working class is hardly better, he feels that the only hope lies in protecting the relationship he has with Connie and retreating from the world.

10

Towards the End

At the beginning of his literary career, Lawrence had reviewed Thomas Mann's *Death in Venice*, describing its author as 'the last sick sufferer of the complaint of Flaubert', someone, he claimed, who 'stood away from life as from a leprosy'.[1] Perhaps because he falsely assumed that, like that novella's protagonist, Mann was nearing the end of his life, Lawrence seems not to have followed his subsequent career or been aware of the publication, in 1924, of *The Magic Mountain*, an absorbing account of a group of TB sufferers in an Alpine sanatorium. Yet he himself was now willing to test again the possibly magic effect of mountain air by joining both Huxley and his brother Julian when, with their wives, they decided to take a skiing holiday in the Swiss resort of Les Diablerets. Although he was in no condition to ski himself, he had plenty to occupy his time as he dealt with the chaotic preliminaries of publishing *Lady Chatterley's Lover* (Orioli's printer knew no English), sent out subscription forms and kept a careful eye on the money coming in. Anxious at first that there would not be enough to cover his costs, he quickly became aware that there would be no such danger, and it was not long before he was all of £1,000 in the clear.

Back in the Villa Mirenda in March 1928, Lawrence carried on with his paintings, encouraged by an invitation from Dorothy Warren, one of Barby's friends, to exhibit them in the London gallery she ran with her husband. In May, the lease on the Villa Mirenda was due to run out, but Lawrence extended it for another six months because Frieda was happy there and getting *Lady Chatterley* into print was taking longer than expected. Apprehensive of the summer heat, the Lawrences nevertheless moved towards the mountains again in June, accompanied by the Brewsters, and on 14 June, in a hotel not far from Grenoble, they had an unpleasant experience. They had all four decided that the hotel they had chosen was ideal – sufficiently high up yet surrounded with flat areas where Lawrence could walk – but on the following morning, he found the consensus had suddenly changed, and the others told him that they did not after all like the hotel and felt it was time to move on. The reason they kept from him was that the landlord had heard Lawrence coughing during the night and invoked a local bye-law that laid an embargo on TB sufferers; there is no doubt Lawrence understood perfectly well what had gone on and must have realized that he had suffered the same fate as Mansfield in Italy.

From Grenoble, the Lawrence party moved to the high country behind Vevey on the lake of Geneva and then further up to Gsteig, not far from Les Diablerets. The Brewsters found a hotel there while the Lawrences rented a chalet in Gstaad, higher up in the mountains. Its drawback was that the land all around was steep, so that Lawrence was continually made conscious of how failing lung power hindered his mobility. But *Lady Chatterley* had finally emerged from the printers in July, so there was plenty to organize and control on that front, and he had recently begun to write short articles for newspapers and magazines, which his agent in the Curtis Brown London office, Nancy Pearn, was mostly able to sell for between £15 and £25. With the success of his novel, this was money for which he no longer had any pressing need, but, having been poor all his life, he was happy to accumulate some savings at last. Pearn was worried that *Lady Chatterley* would ruin his reputation in the magazine market, but the opposite seems to have been the case, notoriety being as much an aid to crucial name recognition as fame.

Many of the short pieces Lawrence was now writing were autobiographical. A good example would be 'Hymns in a Man's Life', an attractive account of the indelible impression made on him by the Nonconformist hymns of his youth. How indelible is confirmed by Achsah Brewster, who records the way Lawrence

D. H. Lawence with his older sister Emily, 1928.

could make the time of a tedious rail journey pass by leading them in a rendition of 'Throw out the lifeline, someone is drowning today'. This was a favourite of the Band of Hope temperance society, whose members would sing it outside public houses, dressed as lifeboatmen; Lawrence, who knew 'every word of every verse', would, like them but in a more ironic vein, accompany his singing with actions suggestive of pulling strenuously on a rope as he hauled in drowning souls.[2]

At one point in 'Hymns in a Man's Life', Lawrence quotes lines from a hymn, which read, 'Fair waved the golden corn/ In Canaan's pleasant land' and comments, 'I love Canaan's pleasant land . . . The wonder of Canaan' which could never be localized. He goes on: 'I should have missed bitterly a direct knowledge of the Bible, and a direct relation to Galilee and Canaan, Moab and Kedron, those places that never existed on earth.' This is the imaginary biblical world of his youth, which he recreates so well in a novella he began writing shortly after his Etruscan tour and which became *The Man Who Died*. Dealing as it does with the Resurrection, and quite specifically the resurrection of the body, this novella opens with a vividly evocative account of what it might feel like to be coming back from the dead (an experience that recent health problems had given Lawrence ample qualifications to describe). Still fragile and tender, the resurrected Jesus figure is surrounded by a harsh and hostile world until he has the good fortune to meet a princess who has become a priestess of Isis. In the ancient Egyptian fertility myth, the task of Isis is to gather up and reanimate the scattered body parts of her brother Osiris, the genitalia last of all. The gentle ministrations of the priestess to the still-wounded man, who has recently suffered so much, restore both his health and potency and culminate in her having sex with him. That Jesus should have been a virgin had increasingly been seen by Lawrence as a weakness of Christianity, and in this delicately written story he remedies that defect with a contribution from one of the several rival belief systems to which for years he had been strongly attracted.

Lawrence was disappointed that Gstaad failed to have the same positive effects he believed he had felt during and after Les Diablerets and, in September, he accompanied Frieda to Baden-Baden. From there, she went on to deal with the few possessions they still had left in the Villa Mirenda, while he travelled with the Brewsters to the South of France, where Aldington had invited the Lawrences to stay with him. This was in a property he had rented on Port Cros, a small island opposite Hyères. Since separating from Hilda Doolittle, Aldington had been living with Arabella Yorke, but now that relationship was under threat from another woman he had invited to Port Cros, Brigit Patmore. A great deal of tension was in the air, and matters were not improved for Lawrence when he discovered that the property Aldington had rented was on the top of a steep hill. To reach the beach involved a long trek down (and then back up), of which in his current state he was not remotely capable.

It seems likely that it was on Port Cros that Lawrence came across incontrovertible evidence, in the form of a letter, that Frieda was having an affair with Ravagli, and that her recent periodic absences were to visit him as well as her mother. To add insult to injury (as it were), she had returned from her latest trip with a bad cold, which Lawrence promptly caught, so that all in all it was not a happy time for him. Aldington would suggest later that the party broke up earlier than anticipated solely on account of anxieties about Lawrence's health and the difficulty of calling in medical treatment from the mainland should his condition have worsened. But the nature of his own relations with Yorke and Patmore, as well as the bad weather which interrupted the boat service from Hyères, were likely to have been strong contributory factors.

Where to go in November 1928 was a puzzle, and the Lawrences settled for nearby Bandol. They found in this quiet coastal fishing village a comfortable hotel called the Beau Rivage (it would be some time before Lawrence realized that this was where Murry and Mansfield had stayed in 1916) and liked it so much that they were there for four months. Now that he was so often confined to bed, or at least obliged to get up late, and often lacked the energy for sustained creative endeavour, Lawrence developed a medium for continuing to express himself which he called 'Pansies' (because the English name for these attractive but unobtrusive flowers could be traced back to the French word for thoughts). Short bursts of what was usually – but by no means always – free verse, these sometimes capture a passing reflection ('The mosquito knows full well, small as he is/ He's a beast of prey./ But after all/ he only takes his bellyful,/ He doesn't put my blood in the bank') or describe some aspect of the natural world. They occasionally comment on social or political issues, or they complain about the prudery that results in censorship. Some of them refer directly to his own current condition. 'I cannot help but be alone', one of them reads, 'for desire has died in me, silence has grown,/ and nothing now reaches out to draw/ other flesh to my own', while the threat of depression is countered with 'I never saw a wild thing/ sorry for itself./ A small bird will drop frozen dead from a bough/ without ever having felt sorry for itself'. Sometimes a thought will develop and become more like what we usually think of as a poem. Of many memorable examples, one is 'Won't It Be Strange – ?':

> Won't it be strange, when the nurse brings the new-born infant
> to the proud father, and shows its little, webbed greenish feet
> made to smite the waters behind it?
> or the round, wild vivid eye of a wild goose staring
> out of fathomless skies and seas
> or when it utters that undaunted little bird-cry
> of one who will settle on ice-bergs, and honk across the Nile?

The second, concluding verse of this poem describes how the dismayed husband asks the woman where this little beast came from, whereupon there is a singing of swans in the heavens which breaks his eardrums and leaves him 'forever listening for an answer'.[3] The background is of course the myth of Leda and the swan, but it is hard not to think also of those passages in *Lady Chatterley* where Clifford encourages Connie to have a child whom he can adopt as his heir and, nurture being so much more important than nature, not to worry about the biological father. But she of course will have none of that (a strong sympathy for maternal feelings is a surprising new feature of *Lady Chatterley's Lover*).

The Lawrences had several visitors while they were at Beau Rivage. These included the Huxleys and the Brewsters, but there were also young admirers of Lawrence, one of whom, an Australian called Stephenson, was especially interested in painting. He arranged to have published a book of the works by Lawrence which Warren was still intending to exhibit in her gallery, and for this Lawrence wrote a 'peppery' introduction, describing how consciousness of the body had been driven out of Europe by fear of syphilis during the sixteenth century. One consequence was that, in subsequent English portrait painting especially, clothes became more of the subject than whatever was inside them. The importance of Paul Cézanne lay in his having been the first to attempt a return to the representation on canvas of outside reality in all the solidity of its actual existence. The then-fashionable doctrine of 'significant form', proposed by critics such as Clive Bell and Roger Fry, seemed to Lawrence to go back to Plato and be concerned with what lies behind nature, whereas, in his view, Cézanne was tormented by the effort to give a truer representation of the here and now, free of the clichés that have grown up over the centuries to impede and distort our vision. Heroic as he was, it was only in his still-life paintings, and particularly in his paintings of apples, that he was successful. Because Lawrence's essay appeared as 'An Introduction to *These* Paintings' (my italics), it might seem to suggest that it had fallen to Lawrence to pick up the baton and paint true representations, not merely of apples but of the human body – yet that title came about accidentally, and, confident as Lawrence usually was about the value of his work, it is extremely doubtful he believed that, with a paintbrush in hand, he had been able to go one better than Cézanne.

Another young admirer who visited Beau Rivage, before as well as after Christmas, was Rhys Davies, whose first novel Lawrence had quite liked and who happened to be living in Nice. Lawrence could complain to him about censorship – one or two of the packages of *Lady Chatterley* he had posted to Britain had been confiscated by the authorities, as had a copy of what had become a whole volume of *Pansies*, even though it had been sent by registered post. Irritating him also was the publishing trade. Because *Lady Chatterley's Lover* had been published privately and abroad, it was not protected by copyright, and its success had led to numerous pirated editions. The only remedies, Lawrence was told, would be either to arrange to have expurgated editions appear in England and the United States, or to undersell the pirates by publishing a cheap edition of his own (as copies of the first Florence edition began to dwindle, he and Orioli doubled the price of the remainder from 2 to 4 guineas). The drawback to this second solution was that it would mean a trip to Paris. Davies volunteered to accompany Lawrence there while Frieda took one of her trips to see her mother. Because it was thought that making the journey in a single day might be tiring, the two men decided to share a hotel room on the way. They set off in March 1929, and, watching Lawrence dry himself after a bath, Davies remembered never having seen 'such a frail, wasted body, so vulnerable-looking'.[4]

Once in Paris, Lawrence met a bookseller who was holding a stash of pirated copies of *Lady Chatterley* and who offered him almost £500 if he would allow a slip to be attached to them which indicated they had been endorsed by the author. It would have saved a lot of trouble, but, as Lawrence said, it is understood that Judas is ready with a kiss but that is no reason for kissing him back. He therefore pursued his negotiations for a cheap edition of his own, which would eventually bring in around £1,200. To it he attached a short preface describing, in a lively and amusing fashion, how pirates had made the edition necessary and calling it 'My Skirmish with Jolly Roger'. When this was later enlarged to the much better known *A Propos of Lady Chatterley's Lover*, he would wander into strange waters.

If he had relied on words like 'cunt' and 'fuck' in writing *Lady Chatterley*, Lawrence claimed in *A Propos*, it was because they were 'a natural part of the mind's consciousness of the body'. Since the apparently increased sexual activity of his time (the 'roaring twenties') was in his view mostly based on feelings that were counterfeit, he declared that the present need was to 'realize' sex more clearly and accurately rather than practise it: 'Ours is the day

D. H. Lawrence, self-portrait, 1929.

of realization rather than of action . . . only fresh mental realization will freshen up the experience.' He had noted how George Bernard Shaw, whom he clearly felt shared the same 'avant-garde' views on sex that he attributes in his novel to Clifford Chatterley's cronies, had scoffed at the pope for insisting that female churchgoers should always be modestly attired, and had moreover added that there would be more profit in asking Europe's chief sex worker for views on sex than its chief priest. But Lawrence defended the pope, and indeed the whole Catholic Church, for having been more successful than its Protestant rivals in the incorporation of essential pagan rituals: 'Oh what a catastrophe for man when he cut himself off from the rhythm of the year ... we are bleeding at the roots, because we are cut off from the earth and sun and stars.' What he finds admirable is that the Catholic Church 'really rests upon the indissolubility of marriage', and he writes several paragraphs in praise of married life, rather forgetting that the novel he is defending deals with adultery. Lyrically describing how, although men and women will both change a good deal during a long married life, they can nonetheless make a symphony of 'soundless singing', he then adds the rider that 'marriage is no marriage that is not basically and permanently phallic' and goes on to claim that 'affinity of mind and personality is an excellent basis of friendship between the sexes, but a disastrous basis for marriage.' *A Propos* is full of controversial and interesting material, but as a defence of *Lady Chatterley's Lover* from a linguistic, moral or literary point of view, it often seems beside the point.[5]

The Huxleys happened to be living close to Paris while Lawrence was there and, anxious about his health, arranged for him to see a doctor who was up to date and had all the latest medical equipment. After a preliminary consultation, Lawrence was persuaded to book an X-ray, but he then cancelled at the last minute. The reason, Huxley suspected, was that the return of Frieda had produced in her husband a temporary improvement. For some time, the Lawrences had been thinking about Spain as a place to visit, and in April, indomitable travellers as they were, they began making their way to Barcelona. From there, they went almost immediately to Majorca and stayed until June, when the exhibition of Lawrence's paintings was due to open in London. They had decided that, since Lawrence did not feel well enough to attend, Frieda should go in his stead and so they parted company in Marseilles, with Lawrence due to join the Huxleys at the seaside resort of Forte dei Marmi, on the Tuscan coast.

D. H. Lawrence in Majorca, 1929.

Frieda enjoyed herself immensely in London. Old friends welcomed her warmly, and the exhibition was a success – until, that is, the police appeared and closed it down by taking away many of the pictures, especially those in which, in defiance of convention, female nudes were shown with pubic hair. Lawrence's problems with censorship had been grumbling away for some time, and the confiscation of his paintings was a step towards open warfare. His friends began organizing protests, but it soon became clear that the pictures would only be returned if he signed an undertaking not to exhibit them in England again. Loath as he was to back down, he preferred that option to having them destroyed. Communications between Italy and London must have been difficult, but they were in any case cut short when Frieda received a telegram from Orioli urging her to return at once. Lawrence, it seemed, had been so ill in Forte dei Marmi that he had been transported back to Orioli's flat in Florence and was now in a state that prompted him to call for Frieda's return.

No medicine was more effective for Lawrence's condition than Frieda. This was partly because he seemed simply to need her to be around in order to feel better, but also on account of her instinctive distaste for the weak and sick which he had dramatized in the figure of Ursula Brangwen. Frieda did not want to be married to an ailing man and supported her husband in his conviction that his problems were temporary and he would one day recover. When the two of them moved to Baden-Baden and then to a village in the Bavarian mountains called Rottach, they were still looking for cures, although now the medical advice was to abandon altitude and get back to the Mediterranean coast. Yet it was while he was in Rottach that Lawrence found the energy to write a pamphlet on the issue of pornography and obscenity, which was published as a response to one called 'Do We Need a Censor?' by William Joynson-Hicks. Denouncing what he felt were the widespread masturbatory tendencies in the current culture and tracking them back to the idea of sex as a 'dirty little secret', Lawrence complained about how difficult it was to tread a path between glib modern reformers and the 'grey elderly ones' of the last century, the century of 'the mealy-mouthed lie', while still maintaining the dynamic character of sex. He offered the recent seizure of his own paintings as an example of foolish censorship and was delighted when his pamphlet outsold that of Joynson-Hicks, who had been the home secretary when friends of Lawrence had raised in the House of Commons the question of the illegal seizure of his copy of *Pansies* by the Post Office.

In September 1929, the Lawrences moved back to Bandol, although this time Frieda, who was tired of hotel life, insisted that they rent a villa. Beau Soleil was modern and about the most architecturally undistinguished dwelling they had ever occupied, but it had central heating, and this was important with winter coming on and Lawrence so often confined to bed. There was the usual stream of visitors, including this time Frederick Carter, whom Lawrence had last seen during his short stay in the Shrewsbury area in January 1924. They would have discussed the Book of Revelation, since Carter's book on that subject was about to come out, accompanied by Lawrence's introduction. But their interpretations differed considerably, and Lawrence felt the need to express his own separately in the last extended piece he was to write. Completed in January 1930, it appeared posthumously in June 1931 under the title *Apocalypse*.

Lawrence had always favoured James Pryse's reading of Revelation as a text about the human body, with the seven seals as references to *chakras* or body centres, in Lawrence's own terms 'the biological psyche'. But in *Apocalypse* this is on the back burner, and he concentrates instead on the idea of it as a palimpsest, the rewriting or adaptation of ancient prophetic writings from well before the time of Jesus (or Plato). What one could glimpse in it, he contended, was a 'secret doctrine' shared by many cultures around the time of Babylon: Chaldean, Persian and also (he could now add) Etruscan. It was this, he argued, which the Jewish writer had adapted for his own purposes. What had made the result so popular among Christians was the addition by its author (John of Patmos rather than the John to whom the fourth gospel is ascribed) of rancorous hatred of the rich and powerful – Romans in his case. In one of the best passages, Lawrence describes how enthusiastically this element of hatred and envy was endorsed by the non-conformist Christians of his youth, especially the Primitive Methodists, for whom the prospect of heaven could not be pleasurable without the accompanying thought of the wealthy burning forever in hell.

Central to Lawrence's reading of the Book of Revelation is the distinction he makes between symbolism and allegory (the latter being much less interesting to him because it involves one-to-one correspondences). He is drawn mostly to those symbols in Revelation that he believes have been inherited from the pre-Socratic, pre-Christian world. If, as he assumes, they were widely understood, and became part of a universal language, it was because they belonged to the kind of collective unconscious Jung had talked about. In this ancient world, as Lawrence liked to imagine it, people thought in images. In *Fantasia* he had taken some trouble to describe how the image of the mother becomes imprinted on the baby's mind, but he had not then explained how a succession of images could constitute what we call thought, nor distinguish what different kinds of 'thought' there are. Neither does he do either of these things in *Apocalypse*, where he is still locked in the paradox of denouncing words and reasoning, as being against emotional awareness, while still exhibiting great power over both.

Another visitor to Bandol in January 1930 was Andrew Morland, a doctor in charge of the treatment of TB patients at the Mundesley sanatorium on the Norfolk coast. Mark Gertler had been one of his patients there, and, knowing that Morland was about to travel to the South of France, asked if he could find the time to visit Lawrence. Since he and Morland were friends, he probably had less trouble getting the doctor to agree to this visit than those around Lawrence had in persuading him to accept it. But on 22 January 1930, Morland came to Bandol to examine him. He felt that, all things considered, the lungs, although badly scarred, were not too bad – but he was alarmed by Lawrence's general physical state, the obvious sign of which being his weight. This had gone down to 45 kilograms (90 lb), which for a man of about 175 centimetres (5 ft 9 in.) was dangerously low. In his time there was no effective cure for TB, so treatment usually consisted of building up the strength of a patient in the hope of spontaneous remission. Morland spoke of a sanatorium he knew in Vence, a small hill town behind Nice, where the regime was appropriately lax and where Lawrence might usefully spend some time. No doubt aware of how difficult it was becoming to look after him, Lawrence began his journey there on 6 February, accompanied by Frieda and Earl Brewster. At the station of Antibes, they were met by an artist friend of Barby's with his car and driven the rest of the way to Vence; on arrival, Lawrence was so worn out by the journey that he had to be carried into the Ad Astra, as the sanatorium was somewhat ominously named.

D. H. Lawrence memorial, Westminster Abbey.

Over the past several months, he had continued to write poetry, expressing his dismay over the seizure of his paintings and other matters that annoyed him, in angry squibs he thought it appropriate to call 'nettles' rather than 'pansies'. But there were also longer poems which related to his own condition, several of which (such as 'The Ship of Death' and 'Bavarian Gentians') have a memorable and moving resonance. Another is called 'Shadows' and expresses Lawrence's desperate hope that he will be able to participate in the annual cycle of renewal. 'And if, in the changing phases of man's life/ I fall in sickness and in misery', this poem ends:

> my wrists seem broken and my heart seems dead
> and strength has gone, and my life
> is only the leavings of a life;
>
> and still, among it all, snatches of lovely oblivion, and snatches of renewal
> odd, wintry flowers upon the withered stem, yet new, strange flowers
> such as my life has not brought forth before, new blossoms of me –

The memorial to D. H. Lawrence at Kiowa Ranch.

Frieda Lawrence with Dorothy Brett and Mabel Luhan in New Mexico after Lawrence's death.

> then I must know that still
> I am in the hands of the unknown God
> he is breaking me down to his own oblivion
> to send me forth on a new morning, a new man.[6]

But there was no renewal in the Ad Astra. Because Lawrence felt he was getting worse rather than better, he persuaded Frieda to rent a villa in Vence and, on 1 March, have him moved there. She was then able to share the burden of caring for a very sick man with the Huxleys, who were living close by and came to help. Mabel Luhan remembered that Lawrence had once complained to her that no one could know what it was like to have Frieda's 'heavy German hand' on him when he was sick, but now he took comfort from Maria Huxley, whose hands, he said, were like his mother's.[7] Yet Frieda clearly did her best, and it was she who was with him when he died, holding on to his left ankle after Lawrence had drifted into the coma that a morphine injection had eventually induced. This was on 2 March 1930, when – since he had been born on 11 September 1885 – he was still only 44.

The death of Lawrence provoked reactions worldwide. Apart from an insistence on his modest social origins, what characterized most of them is suggested by the title of a biography Aldington would publish in 1951, *Portrait of a Genius, But* . . . The genius tag had pursued Lawrence from the start. In a reminiscence of his beginnings as a writer, in which he talks warmly of Hueffer and acknowledges how much his early support counted, Lawrence noted wryly that in those days many people were inclined to call him a genius as if they wanted to console him for not sharing their own incomparable, middle-class advantages. One might consider how helpful it was to either Lawrence's future reputation or his sense of self to be called a genius so early in his career. Leaving this aside, the formula Aldington echoes with *Portrait of a Genius, But* . . . is a strange one, given how hard it is to think of any overall estimation of a great writer's life and works (those of Joyce or T. S. Eliot, for example) taking place in the absence of qualifications – a fact recognized by our ancestors in their fondness for the idea that even Homer sometimes nods. Perhaps it is therefore worthwhile to keep in mind two observations of Lawrence himself. The first comes when, towards the end of his struggle to work out what he finally felt about Magnus, he writes, 'Even the dead ask only for *justice* . . . Who dares humiliate the dead with excuses for their living?' The second is in his final novel, when he is describing how fascinated Clifford is by all the Tevershall gossip Mrs Bolton brings him and has Connie think, 'After all, one may hear the most private affairs of other people, but only in a spirit of respect for the struggling, battered thing any human soul is.'[8]

References

1 Lawrence before Frieda

1. D. H. Lawrence, 'Enslaved by Civilization', in *Late Essays and Articles of D. H. Lawrence*, ed. James T. Boulton (Cambridge, 2004), p. 159.
2. *The Poems of D. H. Lawrence*, ed. Christopher Pollnitz (Cambridge, 2013), vol. I, p. 425.
3. *The Letters of D. H. Lawrence*, vol. I: *1901–13*, ed. James T. Boulton (Cambridge, 1979), p. 190.
4. See Jessie Chambers, *D. H. Lawrence: A Personal Record* (Cambridge, 1981), pp. 116–18.
5. D. H. Lawrence, *The White Peacock*, ed. Andrew Robertson (Cambridge, 1983), p. 222.
6. *Selected Letters of E. M. Forster*, vol. I: *1879–1920*, ed. M. Lago and P. N. Furbank (London, 1983), p. 222.
7. G. H. Neville, *A Memoir of D. H. Lawrence: The Betrayal*, ed. Carl Baron (Cambridge, 1981), p. 83.
8. D. H. Lawrence, *Introductions and Reviews*, ed. N. H. Reeve and John Worthen (Cambridge, 2005), p. 75.
9. D. H. Lawrence, *Lady Chatterley's Lover*, ed. Michael Squires (Cambridge, 1993), pp. 200–201.

2 Turning Point

1. *The Letters of D. H. Lawrence*, vol. I: *1901–13*, ed. James T. Boulton (Cambridge, 1979), p. 415.
2. Ibid., p. 392.
3. Ibid., p. 410.
4. Ibid., p. 421.

5 Ibid., pp. 476–7.
6 See Edward Nehls, ed., *D. H. Lawrence: A Composite Biography* (Madison, WI, 1957), vol. I, p. 215.
7 D. H. Lawrence, *The Prussian Officer and Other Stories*, ed. John Worthen (Cambridge, 1983), p. 48.
8 *The Letters of D. H. Lawrence*, vol. II: *1913–16*, ed. George J. Zytaruk and James T. Boulton (Cambridge, 1981), p. 21.
9 *Letters*, vol. I, p. 469.
10 *The Prussian Officer and Other Stories*, pp. 14–15.

3 *The Rainbow*

1 D. H. Lawrence, *Sons and Lovers*, ed. Helen Baron and Carl Baron (Cambridge, 1992), p. 467.
2 *The Letters of D. H. Lawrence*, vol. II: *1913–1916*, ed. George T. Zytaruk and James T. Boulton (Cambridge, 1981), p. 365.
3 Ibid.
4 Ibid., pp. 320–21.
5 D. H. Lawrence, *The Rainbow*, ed. Mark Kinkead-Weekes (Cambridge, 1989), p. 234.
6 Ibid., pp. 313, 322, 325.

4 Cornwall and *Women in Love*

1 See Edward Nehls, ed., *D. H. Lawrence: A Composite Biography*, 2 vols (Madison, WI, 1957), vol. I, p. 347.
2 D. H. Lawrence, *Twilight in Italy*, ed. Paul Eggert (Cambridge, 1994), p. 146.
3 Ibid., p. 144.
4 D. H. Lawrence, *Women in Love*, ed. David Farmer, Lindeth Vasey and John Worthen (Cambridge, 1987), p. 485.
5 See Mark Kinkead-Weekes, *D. H. Lawrence: Triumph to Exile* (Cambridge, 1996), p. 327.
6 *The Letters of D. H. Lawrence*, vol. III: *1916–21*, ed. James T. Boulton and Andrew Robertson (Cambridge, 1984), p. 141.
7 Lawrence, *Women in Love*, p. 501.
8 Ibid., p. 80.
9 See Nehls, *A Composite Biography*, vol. I, pp. 379, 386.

10 D. H. Lawrence, *Reflections on the Death of a Porcupine and Other Essays*, ed. Michael Herbert (Cambridge, 1988), pp. 37–8.
11 Ibid., p. 51.
12 Lawrence, *Women in Love*, pp. 314, 320.

5 Orphans of the Storm

1 *The Letters of D. H. Lawrence*, vol. III: *1916–21*, ed. James T. Boulton and Andrew Robertson (Cambridge, 1984), p. 265.
2 D. H. Lawrence, *Studies in Classic American Literature*, ed. Ezra Greenspan, Lindeth Vasey and John Worthen (Cambridge, 2003), pp. 168, 14.
3 Ibid., p. 249.
4 Edward Nehls, ed., *D. H. Lawrence: A Composite Biography* (Madison, WI, 1957), vol. I, p. 71.
5 *Letters*, vol. III, pp. 335, 337.
6 Hans-Wilheim Schwarze and John Worthen, eds, *The Plays of D. H. Lawrence* (Cambridge, 1999), p. 430.
7 *Letters*, vol. III, p. 345.
8 D. H. Lawrence, *England, My England and Other Stories*, ed. Bruce Steele (Cambridge, 1990), pp. 161–6.
9 Lawrence, *Studies*, pp. 260, 264–5.
10 William Blake, *Jerusalem*, chapter 1 (plate 10), in *The Poetry and Prose of William Blake*, ed. David V. Erdman (New York, 1970), p. 151.

6 A Busy Time!

1 For a comprehensive account of these exchanges, see Mark Kinkead-Weekes, *D. H. Lawrence: Triumph to Exile* (Cambridge, 1996), pp. 558–64.
2 *The Letters of D. H. Lawrence*, vol. III: *1916–21*, ed. James T. Boulton and Andrew Robertson (Cambridge, 1984), p. 307.
3 See Edward Nehls, ed., *D. H. Lawrence: A Composite Biography*, 2 vols (Madison, WI, 1957), vol. II, p. 26.
4 Kinkead-Weekes, *Triumph to Exile*, p. 561.
5 D. H. Lawrence, *Psychoanalysis of the Unconscious and Fantasia of the Unconscious*, ed. Bruce Steele (Cambridge, 2004), pp. 16, 20.
6 D. H. Lawrence, *The Lost Girl*, ed. John Worthen (Cambridge, 1981), pp. 202–3, 233–4.

7 *The Letters of D. H. Lawrence*, vol. I: *1901–13*, ed. James T. Boulton (Cambridge, 1979), p. 459.
8 See Kinkead-Weekes, *Triumph to Exile*, p. 855.
9 Catherine Carswell, *The Savage Pilgrimage* (London, 1981), p. 117.
10 D. H. Lawrence, *The Poems of D. H. Lawrence*, ed. Christopher Pollnitz (Cambridge, 2013), vol. I, p. 316.
11 D. H. Lawrence, *Introductions and Reviews*, ed. N. H. Reeve and John Worthen (Cambridge, 2005), p. 288.
12 D. H. Lawrence, *Aaron's Rod*, ed. Mara Kalnins (Cambridge, 1988), pp. 158–64.
13 D. H. Lawrence, *The Rainbow*, ed. Mark Kinkead-Weekes (Cambridge, 1989), p. 409.
14 Lawrence, *Psychoanalysis of the Unconscious*, p. 168.

7 A Wider World

1 *The Letters of D. H. Lawrence*, vol. IV: *June 1921–March 1924*, ed. Warren Roberts, James T. Boulton and Elizabeth Mansfield (Cambridge, 1987), p. 239.
2 D. H. Lawrence, *Studies in Classic American Literature*, ed. Ezra Greenspan, Lindeth Vasey and John Worthen (Cambridge, 2003), p. 415.
3 D. H. Lawrence, *Kangaroo*, ed. Bruce Steele (Cambridge, 1994), p. 175.
4 *Letters*, vol. IV, p. 286.
5 D. H. Lawrence, *Study of Thomas Hardy and Other Essays*, ed. Bruce Steele (Cambridge, 1985), p. 155.
6 Witter Bynner, *Journey with Genius* (New York, 1951), p. 80.
7 *Letters*, vol. IV, p. 455.
8 Ibid., pp. 480, 483.

8 There and Back

1 D. H. Lawrence, *Letters to Thomas and Adèle Seltzer,* ed. Gerald Lacy (Los Angeles, CA, 1976), p. 106.
2 *The Letters of D. H. Lawrence*, vol. IV: *June 1921–March 1924*, ed. Warren Roberts, James T. Boulton and Elizabeth Mansfield (Cambridge, 1987), p. 528.
3 D. H. Lawrence, *The Fox, The Captain's Doll and The Ladybird*, ed. Dieter Mehl (Cambridge, 1992), pp. 193, 216.

4 Catherine Carswell, *The Savage Pilgrimage* (London, 1981), pp. 210–11.
5 D. H. Lawrence, *The Woman Who Rode Away and Other Stories*, ed. Dieter Mehl and Christa Jansohn (Cambridge, 1995), p. 98.
6 D. H. Lawrence, 'Pan in America', in *Mornings in Mexico and Other Essays*, ed. Virginia Crosswhite Hyde (Cambridge, 2009), p. 155.
7 Lawrence, *The Woman Who Rode Away*, p. 137.
8 D. H. Lawrence, *The Boy in the Bush*, ed. Paul Eggert (Cambridge, 1990), pp. 342–7.
9 Mabel's previously unpublished memoirs indicate that she had contracted syphilis from her husband around this time. See Lois Palken Rudnick, ed., *The Suppressed Memoirs of Mabel Dodge Luhan: Sex, Syphilis and Psychoanalysis in the Making of Modern American Culture* (Albuquerque, NM, 2012). She would not have wanted Lawrence to know this and there is no indication in his letters that he did.
10 Dorothy Brett, *Lawrence and Brett: A Friendship* (London, 1933), p. 132.
11 D. H. Lawrence, *St. Mawr and Other Stories*, ed. Brian Finney (Cambridge, 1983), p. 155.
12 D. H. Lawrence, *The Plumed Serpent*, ed. L. D. Clark (Cambridge, 1987), p. 422. I comment more fully on these extraordinary phrases in my *Love and Sex in D. H. Lawrence* (Clemson, SC, 2015), pp. 116–21.
13 See Forster's BBC radio talk on Lawrence as it appeared in the *Listener* (30 April 1930), pp. 753–4.
14 Brett, *Lawrence and Brett*, pp. 192–3.
15 *The Letters of D. H. Lawrence*, vol. V: *March 1924–March 1927*, ed. James Boulton and Lindeth Vasey (Cambridge, 1989), p. 242.
16 See Frieda Lawrence, *Not I But the Wind* (Santa Fe, NM, 1934), pp. 166–7.
17 D. H. Lawrence, *Reflections on the Death of a Porcupine and Other Essays*, ed. Michael Herbert (Cambridge, 1988), p. 343 (the phrase occurs in the essay called '. . . Love was once a little boy').

9 *Lady Chatterley's Lover*

1 D. H. Lawrence, *The Virgin and the Gipsy*, ed. Michael Herbert, Bethan Jones and Lindeth Vasey (Cambridge, 2005), p. 8.
2 Barbara Weekley, 'Step-daughter to Lawrence. II', *London Magazine*, XXXIII (Oct/Nov 1993), p. 14.
3 *The Letters of D. H. Lawrence*, vol. V: *March 1924–March 1927*, ed. James Boulton and Lindeth Vasey (Cambridge, 1989), p. 390.

4 Sean Hignett, *Brett, from Bloomsbury to New Mexico* (London, 1984), p. 192.
5 Douglas's pamphlet is reprinted in Keith Cushman's edition of Lawrence's introduction to the Magnus memoir (Los Angeles, CA, 1987).
6 Nicola Beauman, *Cynthia Asquith* (London, 1988), p. 287.
7 D. H. Lawrence, *Sons and Lovers*, ed. Helen Baron and Carl Baron (Cambridge, 1992), p. 298.
8 D. H. Lawrence, *Reflections on the Death of a Porcupine and Other Essays*, ed. Michael Herbert (Cambridge, 1988), p. 291.
9 Lawrence's defence of his novel is reprinted in D. H. Lawrence, *Lady Chatterley's Lover*, ed. Michael Squires (Cambridge, 1993), p. 333.
10 D. H. Lawrence, *The First and Second Lady Chatterley Novels*, ed. Dieter Mehl and Christa Jansohn (Cambridge, 1999), pp. 229, 564. (Frieda's remark occurs in the foreword she wrote for the 1944 edition of *The First Lady Chatterley*.)
11 D. H. Lawrence, *Sketches of Etruscan Places and other Italian Essays*, ed. Simonetta de Filippis (Cambridge, 1992), p. 48.
12 Ibid., pp. 48, 54.
13 Virginia Crosswhite Hyde, ed., *Mornings in Mexico and Other Essays* (Cambridge, 2009), p. 66.
14 The writer/doctor was Hans Carossa. See Hans Carossa, *Confessions of a European Intellectual* (New York, 1946), p. 288.
15 *The Poems of D. H. Lawrence*, ed. Christopher Pollnitz (Cambridge, 2013), vol. I, p. 10.
16 Lawrence, *Lady Chatterley's Lover*, p. 202 and (for the night of sensual passion) p. 246.

10 Towards the End

1 D. H. Lawrence, *Introductions and Reviews*, ed. N. H. Reeve and John Worthen (Cambridge, 2005), p. 211.
2 D. H. Lawrence, *Late Essays and Articles*, ed. James T. Boulton (Cambridge, 2004), pp. 128–92.
3 *The Poems of D. H. Lawrence*, ed. Christopher Pollnitz (Cambridge, 2013), vol. I, pp. 380–81.
4 Rhys Davies, *Print of a Hare's Foot* (New York, 1969), pp. 154–5.
5 D. H. Lawrence, *Lady Chatterley's Lover*, ed. Michael Squires (Cambridge, 1993), pp. 308, 320–25.

6 Lawrence, *The Poems*, vol. I, p. 641.
7 Mabel Luhan, *Lorenzo in Taos* (New York, 1932), p. 62.
8 *Introductions and Reviews*, p. 70 and Lawrence, *Lady Chatterley's Lover*, p. 101. For a more comprehensive account of the circumstances surrounding Lawrence's death, see my own *Death and the Author: How D. H. Lawrence Died, and Was Remembered* (Oxford, 2008).

Select Bibliography

The following is a list of Lawrence's major publications, with dates of their first appearance in book form (the place of publication is London unless otherwise indicated).

The White Peacock (1911)
The Trespasser (1912)
Love Poems and Others (1913)
Sons and Lovers (1913)
The Prussian Officer and Other Stories (1914)
The Rainbow (1915)
Twilight in Italy (1916)
Amores (1916)
Look! We Have Come Through! (1917)
New Poems (1918)
Women in Love (New York, 1920)
The Lost Girl (1920)
Psychoanalysis and the Unconscious (New York, 1921)
Sea and Sardinia (New York, 1921)
Aaron's Rod (New York, 1922)
Fantasia of the Unconscious (New York, 1922)
England, My England and Other Stories (New York, 1922)
The Ladybird, The Fox and The Captain's Doll (1923)
Studies in Classic American Literature (New York, 1923)
Kangaroo (New York, 1923)
Birds, Beasts and Flowers (New York, 1923)
St. Mawr and The Princess (1925)
Reflections on the Death of a Porcupine and Other Essays (Philadelphia, PA, 1925)
The Plumed Serpent (1926)

Mornings in Mexico (1927)
The Woman Who Rode Away and Other Stories (1928)
Lady Chatterley's Lover (Florence, 1928)
Collected Poems (1928)
Pansies (1929)
Assorted Articles (1930)
The Virgin and the Gipsy (Florence, 1930)
The Man Who Died (1931); Lawrence's own title for this novella was *The Escaped Clock*, which related to a farmyard incident at its beginning (although not only to that)
Apocalypse (1931)
Etruscan Places (1932)
Last Poems (Florence, 1932)
The Plays of D. H. Lawrence (1933)

The most reliable texts of Lawrence's writings, and the ones I have cited here, are in the Cambridge University Press's edition of his complete works, which began in 1980 and has only recently been completed. For details of his life, readers should go first to the Cambridge edition of his letters and then perhaps to the Cambridge biography in three separate volumes by John Worthen (*The Early Years*), Mark Kinkead-Weekes (*From Triumph to Exile*) and David Ellis (*Dying Game*). For those who find their 2,350 pages too much, there are several single-volume biographies by Harry T. Moore (New York, 1954 and 1974), Brenda Maddox (London, 1994), John Worthen (London, 2005) and Andrew Harrison (Chichester, 2016). Extracts from those who recorded their impressions of Lawrence during his lifetime and after his death can be found in the three volumes of Edward Nehls's *D. H. Lawrence: A Composite Biography* (Madison, WI, 1957–9). The critic who did most for Lawrence's reputation in Britain in the years following his death was F. R. Leavis. Since his time, innumerable essays and monographs on almost every conceivable aspect of his writing have appeared in Britain, the United States and elsewhere. Those in search of bibliographic details could consult the 'Further Reading' sections in Andrew Harrison, ed., *D. H. Lawrence in Context* (Cambridge, 2018), Catherine Brown and Susan Reid, eds, *The Edinburgh Companion to D. H. Lawrence and the Arts* (Edinburgh, 2020) or the Bloomsbury *Handbook to D. H. Lawrence*, edited by Annalise Grice and published in 2024, although there are lengthy bibliographies in many similar collections. Among the more recent contributions, John Turner's *D. H. Lawrence and Psychoanalysis* (London, 2020) is perhaps especially worthy of note because it deals with an important topic very few have previously had the necessary expertise to handle competently, while the favourable reception of Francis Wilson's *Burning Man: The Ascent of D. H. Lawrence* (London, 2021) and Lara Feigel's *Look! We Have Come Through!* (London, 2022) suggest there might be a mini revival in Lawrence's reputation after the body blows it received from a long succession of feminist writers, beginning with Kate Millett in her *Sexual Politics* (New York, 1968). Anyone dismayed by the amount of secondary material on Lawrence can cheer themselves up by reading Geoff Dyer's *Out of Sheer Rage: In the Shadow of D. H. Lawrence* (London, 1997), an eloquent and witty description of how not writing a book on Lawrence can lead to saying many interesting things about him.

Photo Acknowledgements

The author and publishers wish to thank the organizations and individuals listed below for authorizing reproduction of their work.

Author's collection: pp. 6, 8, 10, 13, 14, 26, 36, 47, 56, 65, 94, 98, 104, 113, 115, 120, 132, 135, 144, 146, 162, 168, 170, 176; Library of Congress: p. 112; National Portrait Gallery, London: pp. 34, 74, 88, 148; Shutterstock: pp. 29 (Andrea Berg), 93 (Mateusz Juca), 138 (photogal); courtesy of Walkabout Books (www.walkaboutbooks.net): p. 49; Wikimedia Commons: pp. 45 (Public Domain), 68 (Public Domain), 77 (Public Domain), 84 (Public Domain), 153 (Public Domain), 174 (14GTR/CC BY-SA 4.0), 177 (Vivaverdi/CC0 1.0).